instant Puppet skits

Larry Shallenberger

BIG HAIRY ISSUES
KIDS FACE

We make it easy!
2 CDs of dialogue, sound effects
& music are included!

Group resources actually work!

This Group resource helps you focus on **"The 1 Thing™"**—a life-changing relationship with Jesus Christ. "The 1 Thing" incorporates our **R.E.A.L.** approach to ministry. It reinforces a growing friendship with Jesus, encourages long-term learning, and results in life transformation, because it's:

Relational
Learner-to-learner interaction enhances learning and builds Christian friendships.

Experiential
What learners experience through discussion and action sticks with them up to 9 times longer than what they simply hear or read.

Applicable
The aim of Christian education is to equip learners to be both hearers and doers of God's Word.

Learner-based
Learners understand and retain more when the learning process takes into consideration how they learn best.

Dedications

To my boys, Alexander, Nathaniel, and Cole—no matter what issues you face in life, your God is bigger, and your dad is hairier. Live fear free. To my wife, Amy—thanks for putting up with looking at the back of my head as I wrote these scripts. To Group—thanks for being both a compass and a sanctuary throughout the years. To the staff at Grace—"who'd a thunk" that we could get here from there? God even cares about adults' big, hairy issues. Working with you is a gift from heaven.

Instant Puppet Skits: Big Hairy Issues Kids Face

Copyright © 2004 by Larry Shallenberger

All rights reserved. No part of this book may be reproduced in any manner whatsoever without prior written permission from the publisher, except where noted in the text and in the case of brief quotations embodied in critical articles and reviews. For information, write Permissions, Group Publishing, Inc., Dept. PD, P.O. Box 481, Loveland, CO 80539.

Visit our Web site: **www.grouppublishing.com**

Credits
Editors: Mikal Keefer and Amy Nappa
Chief Creative Officer: Joani Schultz
Copy Editor: Patty Wyrick
Art Director/Print Production Artist: Joyce Douglas
Illustrator: Eldon Doty
Cover Art Director: Bambi Eitel
Cover Designer: Illustrated Alaskan Moose
Cover Photographer: Daniel Treat
Cover Puppet by: www.monsterpuppets.com
Production Manager: Peggy Naylor

Unless otherwise noted, Scripture taken from the HOLY BIBLE, NEW INTERNATIONAL VERSION®. Copyright © 1973, 1978, 1984 by International Bible Society. Used by permission of Zondervan Publishing House. All rights reserved.

Library of Congress Cataloging-in-Publication Data
Shallenberger, Larry, 1968-
    Instant puppet skits : big hairy issues kids face / by Larry
Shallenberger.-- 1st American paperback ed.
    p. cm.
    ISBN 0-7644-2691-5 (pbk. : alk. paper)
    1. Puppet theater in Christian education. I. Title.
BV1535.9.P8S52 2004
246'.725--dc21
                                                                    2003025978
10 9 8 7 6 5 4 3 2 1   13 12 11 10 09 08 07 06 05 04
Printed in the United States of America.

Contents

Introduction 6

Top 40 Blues *Sadness* (JOHN 11:32-35) 15
A radio caller works through his blues on air with the "help" of a DJ.

It's No Picnic *Body Image* (PSALM 139:14) 23
Sally and Tom wrestle with body image as they compare themselves to other picnickers.

Hall of Superheroes *Bullying* (PROVERBS 15:1) 29
Several would-be heroes attempt to stop a school bully.

The Not-So-Silent Movies *Self-Control* (2 TIMOTHY 1:7) 37
A high-strung theatergoer must overcome the wiggles.

Test Anxiety *School Pressures* (PHILIPPIANS 4:6-7) 43
Two students face mounting test pressures and an industrial-strength librarian.

Operation Stopwatch *Being Too Busy* (PSALM 131) 49
Our hero is mistaken for a secret agent, and finding leisure time seems like an impossible mission.

Commercial Break *Family Conflicts* (EPHESIANS 5:33) 57
A made-for-television family finds they can't solve their differences.

Canceled *A Parent's Unemployment* (MATTHEW 6:25) 63
The theater company faces unemployment and confronts their anxieties.

Candy Store *Responsibility* (COLOSSIANS 3:23-24) 69
The candy maker's apprentice falls asleep at the wheel. Film at eleven.

The Rescue *Dealing With Differences* (1 SAMUEL 16:7) 75
Our superheroes have their self-esteems unexpectedly rescued.

Scene From an Amusement Park *Fear of Abandonment*
(JOSHUA 1:5B) 81
Lost in an amusement park, Edgar is convinced that his friends have forgotten him.

Contents

Emergency Meeting of the Tree Frog Club *New School and New Friends* (JOSHUA 1:9B) 85
> A neighborhood club faces transition as they lose an old friend and make a new one.

Skating Party of One *Loneliness* (MATTHEW 26:40) 91
> Anthony wrestles with feelings of loneliness while trying to stay on his feet in a rolling throng.

Crowded House *Feeling Replaced by a Baby* (GENESIS 21) 95
> The theater troupe watches a baby, and suddenly Fritz feels like an extra.

Boo! *Fear of the Dark* (MATTHEW 14:22-33) 101
> A sleep over is haunted by overactive imaginations and the "Legend of Big Toe."

Playground Sports Central *Being Picked Last* (ROMANS 12:6-8) 107
> A live broadcast of a pickup game of kickball shows how it feels to be picked last.

Improv at the Cafeteria *Being Ridiculed* (EPHESIANS 4:29-32) 113
> The school cafeteria has become a comedy club, and everyone is struggling *not* to be the punch line.

A Mouthful of Fear *Fear of Dentists and Doctors* (ISAIAH 41:10) 119
> An urban legend about a sadistic dentist creates a world of trouble for a toothache sufferer.

Holed Up *Fear of War and Terrorism* (PSALM 46:1) 125
> The Tree Frog Club learns of a terror alert and takes action. Anyone know how to mix cement?

Homecoming *Parents* (EPHESIANS 6:1-2) 133
> Norton struggles to get along with his adult parents and has to look for "expert" advice.

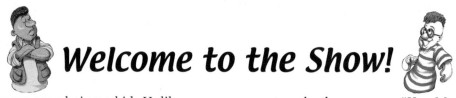

Welcome to the Show!

It's not always easy being a kid. Unlike an amusement park, there are no "You-Must-Be-This-Tall-to-Ride" signs that prevent small souls from stepping on the wild rides of parents' divorce, bullying, or the fear of war. You want to let kids know that God can help them deal with life's challenges. First you'll need the children's permission to enter their world. But how? Introduce the child to a puppet. Puppets provide a humorous and safe way for a child to explore tough emotional issues in a low-risk manner.

The twenty scripts you'll find in *Instant Puppet Skits* have something in common: Each script addresses an issue that research shows is one of the most prevalent issues that children face. And you'll find that the scripts have other things in common too:

- Each script provides a way to involve the audience. Sometimes they'll have a part in the skit, and other times they'll provide a sound effect or a prop.

- After each script you'll find questions designed to help children apply what they've experienced and brainstorm Biblical responses to life's big, hairy issues.

- Scripts have no more than four puppets on stage at any one time, and usually far fewer. That makes it easy for you to recruit enough puppeteers!

- And each script is already recorded on a fun soundtrack. You and your puppeteer friends don't have to worry about digging up sound effects or reading the lines as you perform. It's already done for you!

WHAT TO DO IF A CHILD IS REALLY AFFECTED BY A SKIT

You are holding a potent book. Each of the twenty big, hairy issues of life represented in this book was chosen based on research that shows these are important issues for children. Pick any skit in this book and chances are, at least one of the children in your church is dealing with that big, hairy issue right *now*.

These skits have a strong relational and interactive piece in them, which adds to the power of the scripts. As children connect with both puppets and peers, they won't just think about the topic...they will *feel* the subject matter.

Some of these feelings might be overwhelming to the child. A child might start to cry, or withdraw, or even share strong personal experiences. Here are some tips to help a child navigate his or her way through an unexpected meltdown:

Be shock proof. A look of horror on your face tells a sharing child that he or she is bad and the situation is beyond repair. Stay calm and supportive, no matter what you are feeling.

Create a sense of safety. Don't allow other children to snicker or make fun of the emotional child. Not only will that child stop sharing, but also the other children will know that it's not safe to be vulnerable in the future.

Know your limits. If you aren't sure how to help a child, it's OK to get help. Ask your pastor for a list of counselors that you can refer a family to if a child is in crisis.

Report suspected incidents. If you *suspect* that a child has suffered or is suffering physical or sexual abuse, federal law *requires* you to report the incident. Most states' Department of Child Welfare sponsors a confidential hot-line number to which you can report the suspected incident. Don't know who to call? Visit www.childhelpusa.org. This Web site catalogs reporting procedures and phone numbers for all fifty states. In Canada, contact your local Child Welfare agency. If a child shares about an incident of abuse with you, listen but don't ask leading questions. Immediately report the incident to the authorities and the leadership of your church.

HOW TO PERFORM A PUPPET SKIT

1. RECRUIT PUPPETEERS.

Involve children every chance you have! Maybe your performance production values will suffer, but the learning your children experience more than makes up for the occasional missed exits and entrances.

2. CREATE A STAGE.

You can get by with a table turned on its side, but you'll be more comfortable and provide better performances if you design a puppet stage that includes these elements:

- an elevated stage area,
- side panels,
- lighting controls (so you can dim the stage lights), and
- a backstage pad to save wear and tear on your puppeteers' knees.

See the diagram on next page for an example of how to create a simple stage.

3. SELECT A SKIT.

Listen to the CD, and then assign roles to specific puppets and puppeteers. In the table of contents of this book, you'll also find Scripture references for each skit to help you select which skits will fit into your upcoming programs.

4. COLLECT PROPS AND BUILD SETS.

These skits are intentionally prop and set "light," so you'll need very few items.

5. PRACTICE, PRACTICE, PRACTICE.

See "A Puppet Primer" (p. 8) for a short list of skills you'll want your puppeteers to master. Also make certain puppeteers are familiar with specific scripts before performing them—including lines, emotions, blocking, and entrances and exits.

6. BREAK A LEG!

Perform your show! Use the prerecorded soundtrack, or work without it—it's your choice!

Allergy Alert

Some of the activities in this book use food. Be aware that some children have food allergies that can be dangerous. Know your children, and consult with parents about allergies their children may have. Also be sure to carefully read food labels, as hidden ingredients may cause allergy-related problems.

Teacher Tip

During the performances, children are often asked by the puppets to discuss a question. The CD recording allows children about thirty seconds for discussion. If you find that children are engaged and need longer to complete this time of sharing, simply pause the CD until they're ready to move on.

Staging Terms

We use simple stage instructions to help you move the puppets. You'll want everyone on your team to know these terms so that, during rehearsals, it's easy to communicate where you want puppets to move.

STAGE TERMS

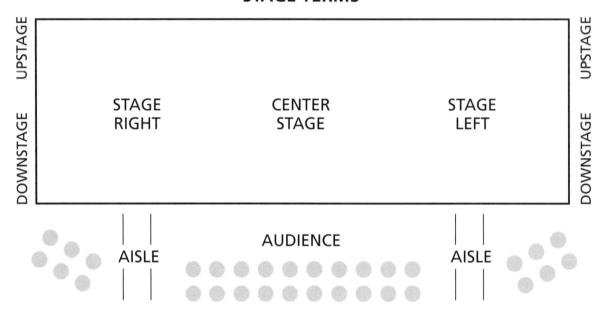

Costuming on a Budget

Keeping your puppets in clothing doesn't need to be expensive. First, experiment with children's clothes until you discover what size each of your puppets wears. Advertise a clothing drive in your church bulletin. Soon you'll have a wide variety of costumes for your puppets. Avoid "dated" clothing, as you want every detail of your puppet scripts to promote a sense of connection to the world of today's kids.

A Puppet Primer

The best thing about working with puppets is that puppets grab children's imaginations. When you're leading a puppet show, you aren't just sending your puppets scampering across a makeshift stage in the corner of your room. You're also playing on the grand stage of your children's imaginations.

With a twist of your wrist, you can convince children that a large, talking, purple dog has hit a home run. Your nimble fingers can send a marionette tap-dancing across a fairy-tale carpet of flowers. Lowering a simple yellow disk on a stick to show the sun setting can be enough to cause droopy eyes.

A good puppet show connects with kids in a way that's powerful and effective, so you want to do it well.

Whether you're a solo artist who's just beginning or you direct a team of experienced puppeteers, there are disciplines you'll want to master. Why? Any puppeteer who has dropped a prop or forgotten to come in on cue knows how fast a group of children will zero in on a mistake. Those distractions take away from the fun, the imagination, and, most important, the message.

To keep children focused on the message, practice the following skills until your puppets shine.

LIP-SYNC WITH PRECISION.

If you're using puppets with moving mouths, be careful to minimize the amount of mouth movement. When people speak, it's primarily the lower jaw that moves. When your puppets speak, simulate the same movement. Use your thumb to move the lower jaw of your puppet, and don't open the mouth wide unless you want your puppet to show surprise.

IMPROVE PUPPET POSTURE.

Puppeteering is hard work! It's tempting to relax a bit by letting your arm drift down, especially if you're working behind an elevated stage and you have to keep your arms above your head.

Always keep your arms at a ninety-degree angle to the floor. The characters you're portraying wouldn't walk leaning over, so don't let them. Some puppeteers use a slight bobbing motion to simulate running when puppets dash from one place to another. It's a good technique, but if you use it, be sure *everyone* in your puppet troupe uses it for consistency's sake.

One thing to keep in mind if you're developing a puppet troupe: The puppeteers must have the upper body strength to keep puppets upright.

LOOK DIRECTLY AT YOUR AUDIENCE.

These scripts call for occasionally addressing your audience directly. When you do so, be sure to make direct "eye contact" by having your puppets "look" directly at the children. If children are seated on the floor, or your stage is high, make the appropriate adjustment by angling your wrists.

KNOW WHAT'S IN VIEW.

Raise your arm too high and it's painfully obvious that Norton doesn't have feet—he's walking around on a forearm. Not good.

Practice makes perfect. And if you're able, consider having a monitor hooked up to an inconspicuous video camera that's out in front of the stage. Place the monitor where your puppeteers can see it as they perform. But be careful; this technique may be distracting and create more problems than it solves.

BE ABLE TO MAKE A GRACEFUL ENTRANCE AND EXIT.

When making entrances and exits, be consistent about whether you let puppets "stair-step" (move up and down as if climbing or descending steps) at the edge of the stage or whether they'll move off stage fully standing.

An easy way to resolve the situation is to build a stage that features side panels with ample room for puppeteers to move puppets out of sight before dropping them below the audience's sightline.

KNOW YOUR SCRIPT.

Certain Shakespearean actors might disagree, but we think puppet plays may be more challenging than people plays, and here's why:

Puppets can't read the audience. When you're doubled over with both arms high over your head, wondering how you'll sneak past another puppeteer so your puppets can cross the stage and exit, you can't see how the audience is responding. You have to rely just on what you hear. When the audience unexpectedly laughs, it may be because you were brilliant delivering a line…or because a puppet's head just fell off.

Having whatever script you're using down cold lets you pay attention to the details that can turn a good performance into a great one.

Know the lines. Know the blocking. Practice stage movement.

Trim Your Cast—and Cut Costs

Something you'll quickly discover about puppets: They can be pricey. Even when you create your own, you'll find that they're expensive to make and maintain.

Here's a way to trim the number of puppets you'll need for these skits: Create an *ensemble cast*. That is, always use one puppet to play the part of a bumbling sidekick, another to be the female lead, and another to play the director or hero.

Creating an ensemble cast is a strategy that has served Jim Henson Productions and the Muppets well.

Think about it: Kermit the Frog plays many different roles throughout the Muppet movies and television programs, but he's always essentially the same character: the reasonable, calm, "Everyman" who finds himself surrounded with more colorful characters. Miss Piggy is always the self-possessed prima donna, and Fozzie is always the scattered, hyper, kindhearted sideman.

We've provided a recommended cast list for you to use if you want to keep your puppets' characters consistent as you present these scripts. Doing so lets you do all these scripts with just a few puppets.

Note: The price of this text includes the right for you to make as many copies of the skits as you need for your immediate church performing group. If another church or organization wants copies of these skits, it must purchase *Instant Puppet Skits: The Big Hairy Issues Kids Face* in order to receive performance rights.

NORTON

EDWARD

SUE

FRITZ

The four primary puppet characters you'll need if you create an ensemble include:

Norton is a levelheaded character who doesn't panic, even in the midst of chaos. He's the perfect narrator or leader, though he's not used to anyone in the ensemble cast actually following him.

Edward has played Macbeth and is a serious thespian. He regards himself a bit above the novices he has been reduced to acting alongside, but the show must go on. Prone to occasional tantrums, he has been known to sulk in his dressing room. He's capable of brilliance on stage but not as often as he imagines.

Sue is a strong, caring character who is self-aware and able to speak with certainty. Her melodic voice makes her a great narrator. She's steady and aware, a character who moves with purpose and conviction.

Fritz is easily excited and eager to please, but he seldom has a complete grasp on what's happening around him. He tends to move about quickly and is perfect as comic relief.

If you create an ensemble, here's how they can fit with the skits in this book:

TOP 40 BLUES

DJ Dazzle: Sue

Al Bum: Fritz

Clyde: Norton

IT'S NO PICNIC

Sally: Sue

Tom: Fritz

HALL OF SUPERHEROES

Cafeteria Man: Edward

Gentleness Guy: Fritz

Super Glue: Sue

Boy's Voice: Offstage Voice

THE NOT-SO-SILENT MOVIES

Movie Usher: Norton

Movie Patron 1: Edward

Movie Patron 2: Fritz

TEST ANXIETY

Norton

Mallory: Sue

Scott: Edward

Librarian: Fritz

OPERATION STOPWATCH

Jack: Fritz

Courier: Norton

COMMERCIAL BREAK

Director Norton: Norton

Sue

Edward

Fritz

CANCELED

Sue

Edward

Fritz

CANDY STORE

Chief Candy Maker: Sue

Assistant Candy Maker: Fritz

THE RESCUE

Cafeteria Man: Edward

Super Glue: Sue

Norton

Calvin: Fritz

SCENE FROM AN AMUSEMENT PARK

Edgar: Edward

Woman: Sue

Man: Fritz

EMERGENCY MEETING OF THE TREE FROG CLUB

Paulo: Edward

Kipp: Norton

Rico: Fritz

Molly: Sue

SKATING PARTY OF ONE

Anthony: Norton

Skaters 1 and 2: Fritz and Edward

DJ Dazzle: perky DJ contributing from
offstage

CROWDED HOUSE

Edward

Sue

Fritz

BOO!

Alex: Edward

Dan: Norton

Seth: Fritz

Sue

PLAYGROUND SPORTS CENTRAL

Reporter: Norton

Ollie: Edward

Mia: Sue

Donovan: Fritz

IMPROV AT THE CAFETERIA

Cafeteria Worker: Edward

Fast Freddie: Norton

Silly Sally: Sue

A MOUTHFUL OF FEAR

Norton

Zippy: Fritz

Max: Edward

Alice: Sue

HOLED UP

Kipp: Norton

Rico: Fritz

Molly: Sue

Grandpa Leo: Edward

HOMECOMING

Norton

Pa: Edward

Ma: Sue

OK. You are almost ready.
Just one last thing. Grab any
puppet. Now reach your hand in
and move the puppet's arms and mouth.
Now pray and ask God to move in you the same
way you are moving in the puppet. Pray that God
would animate you and your puppet team. Pray
that God would use your efforts to make
children laugh and that children would learn
that God meets them in their big, hairy needs.

**May God indeed bless you
and animate you.**

Top 40 Blues

Sadness: *John 11:32-35*

Cast:

> **DJ DAZZLE:** a perpetually positive pop radio personality
>
> **AL BUM:** a hard-working assistant to Dazzle
>
> **CLYDE:** a melancholy caller

Costuming: All characters wear present day street clothes.

Props: Two copies of the microphone on page 22, poster board, a sign that reads "All Day, All Night: The Happy Music Station"

Setup: Before the skit begins, make two copies of the microphone picture on page 22. Glue the pictures to a piece of poster board, and cut out the pictures. Tape each microphone on opposite sides of the puppet stage. Tape the sign to the stage area.

SCRIPT

ACTIONS	WORDS
Play track 1 on CD A. DJ Dazzle and Al Bum enter and move to STAGE CENTER.	**DJ DAZZLE** **(Energetically)** And those were the sounds of the band "Frighteningly Happy." I'm DJ Dazzle, and I'm playing your favorite happy hits. Remember we play the "Soundtrack of Your Smile." I'm going to open the telephone lines and let my friend and sidekick, Al Bum, take your requests. **AL BUM** **(Energetically, in smooth FM voice)** OK kids, time to let us know what music *you* want to hear on "The Soundtrack of Your Smile." Turn to someone sitting next to you, and tell that person what your favorite song is. I'll listen in while you talk.

Al Bum moves to STAGE RIGHT behind his microphone. DJ Dazzle moves to STAGE LEFT behind her microphone

Note that the audience only hears Clyde's voice from offstage.

Al Bum's mouth drops open in shock.

AL BUM
(**Eagerly in a rough Bronx accent**) Someone's calling. I love it when people call. (**In smooth FM radio voice**) Hello, you've reached "The Soundtrack of Your Smile." What would you like to hear?

CLYDE
(**Downcast**) Well...uhm. I guess it doesn't matter. How about "I'm Gonna Go Eat Worms."

AL BUM
(**Unsure**) I'm not sure I know that one. How does it go?

CLYDE
(**Not confident, singing**) Well, like this...

"Nobody loves me, Everybody hates me,
I'm gonna go eat worms,
Big ones,
Fat ones,
Every little chewy one..."

AL BUM
(**Interrupts. Disgusted**) Yuck! Sorry, can't help you. Gotta go.

DJ DAZZLE
(**Mildly annoyed**) Who was that?

AL BUM
(**Sheepishly, in Bronx accent**) I think it was a prank call. Sorry about that.

Another caller!

DJ DAZZLE
(**Still annoyed**) Well, get the caller to tell you a song we can play!

SKIT ONE:
TOP 40 BLUES

AL BUM

(In Bronx accent) Will do!

Hello? **(Correcting himself, switching to FM voice)** Whoops, hello, "Soundtrack of Your Smile." What would you like to hear?

CLYDE

(Still glum) You *asked* me to sing the song. If you didn't want to play it, you should have said so. I'm feeling sad, and I want to hear a sad song. How about the "Broken Crayon Blues"?

AL BUM

(Pointedly) You *do* know we only play *happy* music, right?

DJ moves to CENTER STAGE and faces Al.

DJ DAZZLE

(Nervously) Al, we're not playing any music! I need a song—*now*! Who are you talking to?

AL BUM

(In Bronx accent) This guy keeps calling in, asking for sad songs. I don't know what to do with him.

DJ DAZZLE

(Authoritatively) Hang up on him!

AL BUM

I did! But he keeps calling back.

DJ Dazzle moves to STAGE LEFT behind her microphone.

DJ DAZZLE

(Frustrated) I'll handle this. Let me talk to him.

AL BUM

OK boss, but I don't think this is a good idea.

(**Switching to FM voice**) Hey, DJ Dazzle wants to talk with you. I'm going to put you on the speakerphone.

Try not to be *too* sad.

CLYDE
(**Sighing through his sentences**) Hi DJ Dazzle. This is Clyde. I'm really down in the dumps. I just want to hear a sad song. They say so much. Can you play "My Dog Caught the Mumps Before She Got Hit by a Bus Blues"?

DJ DAZZLE
We don't play the blues here. Have you tried *listening* to our music? (**Reciting slogan in radio voice**) "We've got the happy beat that'll move your feet…!"

CLYDE
…but I'm sad…

DJ DAZZLE
"Listen for just a day and your blues will go away…"

CLYDE
…and I don't feel like doing anything…

DJ DAZZLE
"…Spin that dial and start your day with a smile…"

CLYDE
(**Agitated**) Stop! Haven't you ever felt sad? I mean are you *really* happy all the time? I bet I'm not the *only* person in your audience who's ever felt sad!

DJ DAZZLE
(**Surprised, pensive**) Has my audience ever felt sad? I've never thought about that…

Tell you what, Clyde, I'll throw the question out to my listening audience. Let's see if they ever feel sad.

Kids in the audience, do you ever feel sad? Turn to the person you were talking with before, and tell your partner about a time when you felt sad. Talk about what you did when you were down in the dumps. While you're talking, I'll play the new happy hit, "Happy, Happy, Smiley, Happy."

DJ DAZZLE
You've got fifteen seconds left to talk… time's up! Now, has anyone here ever felt sad? Raise your hands….

DJ moves to CENTER STAGE and faces Al.

(**Surprised**) What do you know? It seems that many of our callers experience a case of the blues from time to time.

Al Bum, this is going to take some special music. Get me that song, "Happy Puppets!"

Al Bum races OFFSTAGE RIGHT.

AL BUM
(**Excited, in Bronx accent**) Will do!

(**Offstage**) This could take awhile. We don't get a lot of requests for that one…

DJ Dazzle moves back to her microphone.

CLYDE
You know, sometimes people feel sad and it takes more than a happy song to cheer them up.

DJ DAZZLE
How can that be? Haven't you heard that with a happy song in your heart your troubles all fly away?

CLYDE
Look—I'm changing stations. I'll tune back in when I'm feeling happier! You're not helping me at all.

DJ DAZZLE
(**Surprised, to self**) Well...what do you think of that?!

AL BUM
(**Calling from offstage right**) I found the song, boss!

DJ Dazzle turns and faces STAGE RIGHT.

DJ DAZZLE
(**Frantic, calling stage right**) Then get it on the air!

Al Bum dashes back ONSTAGE to previous position.

DJ Dazzle faces her microphone.

DJ DAZZLE
(**Smoothly**) Thanks for joining us, audience! Enjoy this classic hit, "Happy Puppets!"

DJ Dazzle turns from the microphone to talk to Al Bum.

(**Sadly**) Boy, that was awful. A caller who doesn't like happy music. A caller who's *sad*...who says I'm not *helping* him...

AL BUM
Hey, are you...are you *sad*?

DJ DAZZLE
(**Embarrassed**) Me? No—of course not. I just had something in my eye...

Al Bum turns and faces DJ Dazzle and takes a few steps toward her.

(**Recovering, sternly**) Now get back there, and clean up that mess you made! I'm going to take a break while this song plays.

Al Bum backs away.

AL BUM
OK, boss...right away, boss.

Al Bum scampers back off STAGE RIGHT as DJ exits STAGE LEFT.

DJ sticks her head back ONSTAGE and calls to STAGE RIGHT.

(Muttering to self as exits)
I'm sure I saw her crying…

DJ DAZZLE
I heard that!

FOR DEEPER LEARNING

SAY: **Boy, DJ Dazzle has a hard time expressing her feelings. Nobody likes to feel sad, but we all feel sad from time to time. Even Jesus had times of deep sadness.** Read John 11:32-35. **Let's talk about how we can handle our sad feelings.**

Have children form groups of three or four and discuss:

- *How do you cheer yourself up when you feel sad?*
- *Why do you think God lets us feel sad sometimes?*
- *How does God help you when you're sad?*

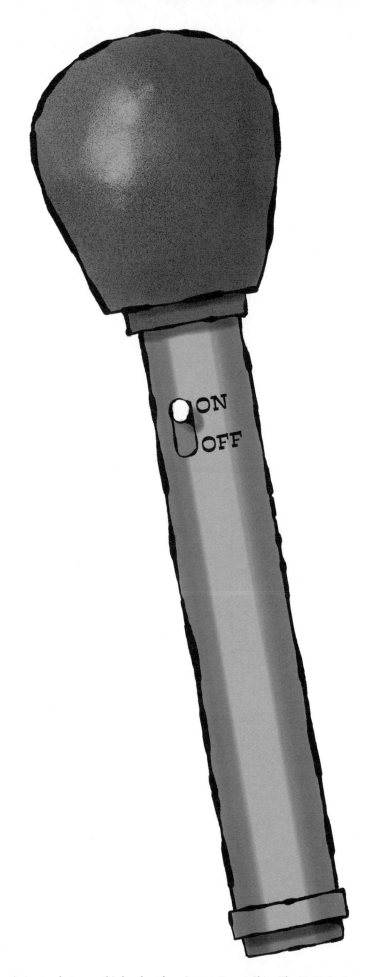

It's No Picnic

Body Image: *Psalm 139:14*

Cast:

> **SALLY:** a little overweight and very insecure about it
>
> **TOM:** blessed with a high-octane metabolism, not the most sensitive guy
>
> **OFFSTAGE VOICE:** announcing the upcoming events

Costuming: All characters wear street clothes.

Props: A sign that reads "School Picnic"

Setup: Tape the sign to the stage area.

SCRIPT

ACTIONS	WORDS
💿 Play track 2 on CD A.	
Sally and Tom enter from STAGE RIGHT and move to STAGE CENTER. Tom looks over his shoulder to STAGE RIGHT and then back to Sally.	**TOM** **(Excited)** Now *this* is a picnic. There are people, music, games, and food! I've eaten forty-seven hot dogs already! Excuse me. I was just complimenting the chef!
Sally faces Tom. Sally looks down at her own body.	**SALLY** **(Resentfully)** Forty-seven hot dogs. I'd turn into a *blimp* if I ate forty-seven hot dogs. **OFFSTAGE VOICE** Five minutes until the pie-eating contest.

Sally takes a step away from Tom and looks down.	**TOM** I'm in! I love pie. So do you, Sally. Care to join me in devouring a dozen pies?
	SALLY (**Quietly**) I've just decided that I don't like pie anymore.
Tom takes a step toward Sally.	**TOM** (**Suspiciously**) Yesterday you said that you love apple pie.
Sally turns her head to STAGE LEFT, then turns to Tom.	**SALLY** (**With hurt tones**) That was before Jackie just said I was chubby. Just look at all the other girls. They're all skinnier than I am.
Tom leans forward, turns his head to STAGE LEFT past Sally.	**TOM** Yeah, those girls *are* skinnier than you are.
Sally lifts and rolls her head emphatically.	**SALLY** *What!?*
Tom faces Sally.	**TOM** What's the big deal? So some girls are skinnier than you are—big deal! Some people are *stronger* than I am. Rafe can throw a football farther. Marcus can drink a whole gallon of lemonade without having to take a bathroom break. *I* can't do that. So you're a little bigger than those girls are. *I* think you're cool.
Sally drops her head.	**SALLY** (**On the edge of tears**) Tommy, you are so *mean*!
Tom moves closer to Sally.	**TOM** (**Clueless**) What did I say? I was just trying to help.

SKIT TWO:
IT'S NO PICNIC

Sally turns her head to Tom.	**SALLY** (**Calming down**) I know you were. (**Sniffing**) You just don't *get* it.
	TOM Get *what*?
	SALLY I'm worried that I won't have enough friends because I'm...I'm...
	TOM ...a little bigger than everyone else?
Sally "stomps" up and down once.	**SALLY** You just don't understand because you're a boy.
Tom inches from Sally a little.	**TOM** I don't understand *what*?
	OFFSTAGE VOICE Seven minutes until the sack races. All contestants report to the soccer field.
Sally takes a few steps STAGE RIGHT, then turns and faces Tom.	**SALLY** (**Perking up**) Do you want to do the sack race together instead? I'd rather exercise than eat. And you *love* to race.
Tom moves STAGE LEFT.	**TOM** I think I'll pass. My racing days are over.
Sally moves CENTER STAGE.	**SALLY** (**Inquisitively**) You *love* to run. You're *always* running. Why don't you want to do the sack race?
Tom turns and faces Sally.	**TOM** That was before Fast Freddie joined our church. That kid is *fast*.
Sally moves next to Tom.	**SALLY** (**Concerned**) *You* used to be the undisputed champion at sprinting.

TOM

(Gloomily) Now I'm yesterday's news. Now they call me "Tom the Turtle." I've tried—but I just can't make my body go any faster.

SALLY

(Sighing) I guess I'm not crazy about my body either.

TOM

I wonder if any of the other kids are happy with everything about their bodies.

Kids, if you had one wish, what one thing would you change about *your* body?

Would you want to be stronger, or thinner, or taller, or faster? Turn to someone near you, and tell that person what you would do with one wish.

Sally and Tom sit dejectedly.

SALLY

(To Tom) I guess most kids would change *something* about themselves if they could.

Sally moves STAGE RIGHT and listens to children.
Sally turns and faces Tom.

TOM

I *hate* picnics. There's *nothing* to do at them.

Tom moves DOWNSTAGE LEFT.

SALLY

(Sighing) At least not for people who are chubby...

TOM

...or slow.

Tom turns and faces Sally.

SALLY

Do you remember the Sunday school lesson this morning? Pastor Ed said that we were "fearfully and wonderfully" made.

Sally moves to CENTER STAGE and looks at Tom.

SKIT TWO:
IT'S NO PICNIC

Tom meets Sally at CENTER STAGE.

TOM

Yeah, I think what Pastor Ed *meant* to say is, **(imitating Pastor Ed's voice—using a lower register of voice)** "Tom, after God made you, he said 'Wonderful. Now I'm frightened. I've made the slowest kid in the world.' "

SALLY

(Laughing a little) I don't think you are that slow. At least you aren't *fat* like me.

TOM

Well I don't think you are all that fat.

SALLY

So you aren't the *fastest* boy in the church. That doesn't mean you have to give up running.

TOM

Well you don't have to give up pie.

OFFSTAGE VOICE

This is the final call for the sack races and the pie-eating contest.

TOM

What are we going to do?

SALLY

I don't want to eat a zillion pies. But I wouldn't mind having one slice. Why don't we do the sack race together? Then we can both have some pie.

Tom moves right next to Sally.

TOM

Sounds good. Let's practice our sack racing.

Tom and Sally exit STAGE RIGHT, bouncing together the whole time.

SALLY

Let's go.

TOM

(Offstage) I can't stop.

SALLY

(Offstage) Me either. And we're headed right toward the…

OFFSTAGE VOICE

LADIES AND GENTLEMEN: I'm sorry to announce that due to an unfortunate accident, the pie-eating contest has been canceled.

FOR DEEPER LEARNING

Read Psalm 139:14. SAY: *God loves the way that he made us. But we don't always agree with God. Sometimes we aren't happy with our bodies. We seem to care a lot about what people think of our bodies! Let's take a look at how we let other people's opinions shape how we feel about ourselves.*

Have children form groups of three or four and discuss:

- *Why do you think Sally and Tom cared so much about what their friends thought about their bodies?*

- *Has anyone ever made fun of how you look or the things that you can do? How did you feel?*

- *What's your favorite part of the way God made you? Why?*

- *Why is it important to pay more attention to how God looks at us?*

SKIT TWO:
IT'S NO PICNIC

Hall of Superheroes

Bullying: *Proverbs 15:1*

Cast:

>**CAFETERIA MAN:** a lunchroom cook turned superhero
>**GENTLENESS GUY:** a swell guy with debatable powers
>**SUPER GLUE:** a novice superhero still mastering her powers
>**BOY'S VOICE**

Costuming: Cafeteria Man, Super Glue, and Gentleness Guy wear street clothes and capes made from bandanas. Cafeteria Man wears a chef's hat.

Props: Three bandanas, a chef's hat, and a sign reading "Hall of Superheroes"

Setup: Pin the chef's hat to Cafeteria Man's head. Tie the bandanas around Cafeteria Man's, Super Glue's, and Gentleness Guy's necks as capes. Hang the sign that says "Hall of Superheroes."

SCRIPT

ACTIONS	WORDS
Play CD A, track 3.	
Cafeteria Man and Gentleness Guy enter from STAGE LEFT and move to CENTER STAGE as they speak.	**GENTLENESS GUY** **(Incredulous)** This is our new headquarters? I don't want to complain, but the old place was *much* nicer. **CAFETERIA MAN** **(Discouraged)** Forgetfulness Girl was in charge of paying the rent on the old place. Three months of late payments and, *Whammo*! We're evicted.
Gentleness Guy looks around while taking a few steps toward STAGE LEFT.	**GENTLENESS GUY** I guess this place will make do for a while. But what's up with the polka music? Why does this place smell like stale spaghetti and meatballs? Pee-ewh!

Cafeteria Man becomes increasingly animated as he reminisces.	**CAFETERIA MAN** **(Sniffing the air)** Spaghetti and meatballs! How I miss the simple days when I was a lunchroom cook! I made children happy by cooking Salisbury steaks and Jell-O. The next day I would make Jell-O with chunks of Salisbury steak suspended inside. **(Pauses.)** Until that fateful day when I was bitten by a piece of radioactive mystery meat. I immediately gained superpowers to plan menus. **(Melodramatically)** I became: Cafeteria Man! **GENTLENESS GUY** Uh, about the polka music?
Cafeteria Man turns his head to STAGE RIGHT, then takes two steps STAGE RIGHT.	**CAFETERIA MAN** **(Calming down)** Oh, *that*. We're renting a banquet room in a wedding hall until we get things straightened out. **(Pauses.)** Did you hear that? A cry for help! **BOY'S VOICE** **(Calling, from a distance)** Help! The bully, Mischievous Max, is threatening to beat me up if I don't write his schoolwork by Monday!
Gentleness Guy moves DOWNSTAGE.	**GENTLENESS GUY** A bully? That's a serious situation. **(To audience)** Kids, have you ever been bullied? Turn to a partner, and tell how you feel when someone bullies you.
Gentleness Guy turns his head and faces Cafeteria Man.	**(To the kids)** That's what I thought. No one likes to be bullied. **(To Cafeteria Man)** I want this mission. You *promised* me that the next mission was mine.

Gentleness Guy moves to CENTER STAGE. Cafeteria Man moves to RIGHT UPSTAGE.

Cafeteria Man shakes his head "no" as he moves to CENTER RIGHT STAGE.

Cafeteria Man turns to OFFSTAGE RIGHT, calling.

Super Glue enters STAGE LEFT.

Cafeteria Man looks down, solemnly.

Cafeteria Man looks up and turns toward Super Glue.

Super Glue tries to move but seems to be stuck to something.

CAFETERIA MAN
(**Hedging**) I said *maybe*. What are your superpowers again?

GENTLENESS GUY
(**Melodramatically**) I have an extraordinary capacity to be gentle. (**In unaffected voice**) That means I'm really good at being kind and loving. Being called mean words doesn't bother me. I just keep showing compassion…

CAFETERIA MAN
Eww! Maybe next time, kid. It's a tough world out there, kid. I don't want to be responsible for you getting hurt. Besides, if the word gets out that one of our heroes got beat up by a grade-school bully, we'll never get that action figure contract. Sorry.

(**Shouting**) We have a situation unfolding at Ridgefield Elementary School. Get Popcorn Boy!

SUPER GLUE
Popcorn Boy is no more. He was crossing a hot pavement and his kernels exploded. He exploded into a four-block-long serving of popcorn. Popcorn Boy died a hot, buttery death.

CAFETERIA MAN
(**Sorrowfully**) Popcorn Boy, you'll be missed. Everyone loves the mouth-watering taste of popcorn.

Super Glue, I'm sending you. You alone have the power to instantly glue that bully to the floor. Hop on your glue stick and ride like the wind!

SUPER GLUE
(Struggling) I can't go. I'm stuck to my chair. You'd better send someone else. I haven't figured out how to control my powers of stickiness.

GENTLENESS GUY
We'll help you!

BOY'S VOICE
He-e-e-e-l-p! Help me!

CAFETERIA MAN
(Hollering) We'll send someone over shortly.

Cafeteria Man and Gentleness Guy push Super Glue off STAGE LEFT.

Cafeteria Man and Gentleness Guy turn and face STAGE RIGHT to listen to the voice.

(To Audience) Kids, we need a plan. Turn to your friend, and talk about ways this boy might handle the bully who is making him write papers. Hurry! We're running out of time!

Cafeteria Man and Gentleness Guy turn and face audience.

GENTLENESS GUY
(To Audience) I heard some good ideas, kids. Thanks! Remember what you were saying—you'll get to talk about it again soon.

CAFETERIA MAN
(With vibrato) Talk? We need *power*—not talk! I'd fight the bully myself… if my arthritis wasn't flaring up. What about Anvil Guy? He could beat up the bully.

Cafeteria Man spins toward Gentleness Guy.

GENTLENESS GUY
(Concerned) Hmmm. If Anvil Guy beats up the bully—wouldn't he be a bully himself?

Gentleness Guy turns and faces Cafeteria Man.

CAFETERIA MAN
(Stammering) Well…I don't know…never thought of that. Isn't it OK to use brute force to defend yourself?

Cafeteria Man turns and faces Gentleness Guy.

Gentleness Guy moves to CENTER STAGE as he talks.

GENTLENESS GUY
If you thought you might be seriously hurt, you could use enough force to protect yourself.

SUPER GLUE
(**Calling**) I can go. I'm almost free.

(**Pauses.**) Just another foot to go. (**Grunting with effort**) Almost…I'm almost there…

Wow, this glue is strong! I think that Gentleness Guy has a point. Maybe the kids can help us.

Cafeteria Man moves DOWN CENTER STAGE to address the audience. Gentleness Guy moves UPSTAGE LEFT.

CAFETERIA MAN
(**Scheming**) The kids, eh? (**Smoothly**) OK kids. You can be junior superheroes and help us out. Naturally, there's a fee involved. It's going to cost each of you $9.95 to join the Official Hall of Superheroes Club. You'll get a membership card and the privilege of giving us advice…

GENTLENESS GUY
(**Shocked**) What are you doing?

CAFETERIA MAN
(**Under his breath, to Gentleness Guy**) What does it look like? I'm trying to make some money. *You're* the one who complained about having our headquarters in a wedding hall.

Gentleness Guy steps forward and turns to Cafeteria Man.

GENTLENESS GUY
(**Admonishingly**) Come *on*! This isn't the way to make money.

CAFETERIA MAN

(Sighing heavily) Fine. **(To children)** Kids, what I was trying to say is that we would be honored if you'd give us some advice. What do you think of this? The boy could tell the bully that if *he* doesn't give the boy five dollars that the boy will tell on him. *That* would fix the bully. Go ahead and talk about it. I'll be listening.

CAFETERIA MAN

You didn't like that idea? OK. Anyone have a better idea?

SUPER GLUE

Here's my idea. The boy could call the bully some mean names. Maybe the bully's feelings would be hurt, and he'd leave the boy alone.

CAFETERIA MAN

Cunning! Kids, what do you think of *this* idea? Sometimes the best defense is a good offense. Show me thumbs up or thumbs down to let me know if this is a good idea.

You think the plan would backfire? You think that the bully would just get angrier? You think the bully might even hit the boy right on the spot?

(Calling offstage) Your idea went nowhere fast, kind of like yourself.

GENTLENESS GUY

(Chuckling to himself over Cafeteria Man's joke)

SUPER GLUE

Very…**(struggling)**…funny. Maybe you have an idea, Gentleness Guy.

Still OFFSTAGE.

Cafeteria Man moves next to Gentleness Guy, talking to Super Glue who is OFFSTAGE over his shoulder.

Guy moves to STAGE RIGHT and faces OFFSTAGE LEFT	**GENTLENESS GUY** (**Collecting himself**) I'm sorry I laughed. I couldn't help myself.
	The kids are right. Calling the bully names will only make things worse.
	OK. Well, I *do* have a few ideas.
Gentleness Guy moves to DOWNSTAGE RIGHT and addresses the children.	(**To kids**) All right kids, what if the boy simply tells the bully, "No. I don't want to write your paper. Leave me alone."
	Turn to a friend next to you and decide if you'd try that approach. I'll wait.
Cafeteria Man moves STAGE LEFT.	**CAFETERIA MAN** (**Reminiscing**) That *is* a tough one! It's like the time I had to fight that batch of nuclear-powered potato salad. I grabbed my spatula and stood my ground. It took a lot of "stick-to-it-iveness." (**Sarcastically**) Super Glue would know about *that*!
	SUPER GLUE Very funny. Would someone help me?
	BOY'S VOICE (**Calling**) I asked *first*. Would someone please help me?
Cafeteria Man turns his head toward STAGE RIGHT.	**CAFETERIA MAN** (**Calling**) Young-boy-whose-name-we-don't-even-know, I'm sending in Gentleness Guy. He'll know how to help you!
	GENTLENESS GUY Thanks, Cafeteria Man. I won't let you down.
GENTLENESS GUY exits STAGE RIGHT.	**CAFETERIA MAN** (**Calling**) Super Glue, I've been saving some grease from the deep fryer for an occasion like this. It's about a month old. I'll pour it on you, and I'm sure you'll slide right off that chair.
Cafeteria Man exits STAGE LEFT as he talks.	

FOR DEEPER LEARNING

SAY: *It's frustrating when someone bullies you. But Gentleness Guy is right.* Read Proverbs 15:1. *A harsh word does only stir up more anger. By calling names or teasing the bully, you only make him angrier. You don't need to let a bully pick on you. Let's talk about some ways that we can handle the bullies in our lives. Let's get into groups of three or four to talk about bullying.* Answer these questions. Ask:

- *Why do you think some people decide to bully?*

- *What are some things that you can gently say to a bully to get that person to stop?*

- *Who can you turn to for help if the bully won't stop picking on you?*

The Not-So-Silent Movies

Self-Control: *2 Timothy 1:7*

Cast:

MOVIE USHER: a dreadfully overworked yet composed employee

MOVIE PATRON 1: a moviegoer with an attention span made for action films

MOVIE PATRON 2: an intelligent movie lover who suffers from impatience

OFFSTAGE VOICE: another moviegoer

Costuming: All characters wear street clothes. If possible, Movie Usher should wear a clip-on bow tie and a vest.

Props: Popcorn popper, popcorn, two small paper bags, coffee filters, and a large sign that reads "Now Showing at Cinema One: *The Secret Lives of Librarians*"

Setup: Before the class, make fresh popcorn for everyone. The coffee filters make great disposable bowls. Affix a small bag of popcorn to the hand of Movie Patron 2, and have one ready for Movie Patron 1. Hang the sign in front of the set. Give each child a bowl of popcorn before the show begins.

> ### Teacher Tip
> *Is letting the children eat popcorn during the puppet script a good idea? Won't the popcorn be a distraction?* One of the points of this script is helping children discover ways to manage their energy and control their "wiggles" during structured teaching times. Research shows that some children actually learn *better* when they have the opportunity to do something quietly with their hands during the lesson.

SCRIPT

ACTIONS	WORDS
Play track 4 on CD A.	
Movie Patron 1 and Movie Patron 2 enter STAGE RIGHT and move to CENTER STAGE.	**MOVIE PATRON 1** So what's this movie about again? **MOVIE PATRON 2** It's a very *important* movie: *The Secret Lives of Librarians.* The movie explores librarians' love affair with the Dewey Decimal System.

MOVIE PATRON 1

How do they work the car chase into the movie?

MOVIE PATRON 2

No car chase. This movie is about people—wonderfully deep, thoughtful people.

MOVIE PATRON 1

I really wanted to see a car chase or an exploding marshmallow factory…

MOVIE PATRON 2

Shhh! The movie is about to begin.

MOVIE PATRON 1

(**Whispering**) All they do is talk. This is *boring*.

MOVIE PATRON 2

Shhh! I'm trying to *listen*.

MOVIE PATRON 1

I'm trying to stay awake. I don't get this movie. Why doesn't anything *happen* in this movie?

MOVIE PATRON 2

(**Annoyed but still whispering**) Shhh! I'm *trying* to enjoy this story.

MOVIE PATRON 1

Story? This isn't a story. *Stuff happens* in a story. I know why this is called the *secret* life of librarians—because no one can stay awake to see what happens at the end.

MOVIE PATRON 2

(**Louder**) Would you *please* be quiet? Shhhh!

Sorry. You see my friend here…

Movie Patron 2 stares ahead attentively, nodding with appreciation. Movie Patron 1 begins to fidget and looks around him.

Movie Patron 2 turns his head toward Movie Patron 1.

Movie Patron 1 looks around to see if anyone else is able to stay awake.

Movie Patron 1 and 2 silently watch the movie.

Movie Patron 1 leans into Movie Patron 2 to ask a question. Movie Patron 2's popcorn spills.

MOVIE PATRON 1

(Whispering) Hold it down. You're going to get us in trouble.

MOVIE PATRON 1

I don't get it. What's going on here...?

MOVIE PATRON 2

(Shouting) Now you've done it. You've spilled my popcorn!

OFFSTAGE VOICE

(Shouting) Would *you* hold it down? We're *trying* to watch this movie.

MOVIE PATRON 2

(Embarrassed) But I...I...I mean he...(Sighs.)

MOVIE PATRON 1

(Whispering) Don't worry. I'll get you a new bag of popcorn. At least I'll get to move around and work out my wiggles.

Movie Patron 1 exits STAGE LEFT while pretending to bump into and climb over several other theatergoers that are between him and the aisle.

Movie Patron 2 watches Movie Patron 1 exit and winces each time he hears someone complain about Movie Patron 1.

Excuse me...
Pardon me...
Pardon *me*...
Watch it...

Movie Patron 2 turns his head forward, sighs, and watches the movie.

Movie Usher enters UP LEFT and moves to DOWN LEFT.

MOVIE USHER

(Politely) Excuse me, sir. Several people have complained about your talking and fidgeting. If you can't control your wiggles, then you'll have to leave.

Movie Patron 2 turns and looks at Movie Patron 1's empty chair.

Movie Patron 1 enters STAGE LEFT with a bag of popcorn.

Movie Patron 1 climbs over several other theatergoers that are between him and his seat.

Movie Patron 2 and Movie Usher both watch Movie Patron 1 struggle to his seat and wince each time they hear someone complain about Movie Patron 1.

MOVIE PATRON 2

Oh no, sir. You have the wrong guy. It's my friend. He just can't sit still. He has no self-control.

MOVIE USHER

I don't see any "wiggly" friend of yours. You're going to have to leave.

MOVIE PATRON 2

(**Stammering**) But, but…

MOVIE PATRON 1

Pardon me…
Excuse me…
Whoops, that stain should come out in the wash…

MOVIE USHER

(**To Movie Patron 2**) Sorry I ever doubted you.

(**To Movie Patron 1**) What seems to be the problem?

MOVIE PATRON 1

I have the wiggles. I *can't* sit still.
(**Whispering to Movie Usher**) No offense, but I don't understand this movie.

MOVIE USHER

(**Whispering to Movie Patron 1**) Neither do I, but I'm not bothering people.
(**Aloud**) Well, you need some self-control. Can you keep your wiggles from bothering others?

MOVIE PATRON 2

(**Loud and irritated**) That's right! You're ruining the movie for everyone.

SKIT FOUR:
THE NOT-SO-SILENT MOVIES

Movie Patron 1 turns to each side and apologizes to the audience.

MOVIE PATRON 1
Sorry...sorry. It won't happen again.

MOVIE USHER
(**To Movie Patron 2**) You need some self-control too. Your anger outbursts are bothering everyone.

(**To children**) Kids, I need your help. What's your best advice that you can give to my fidgety friend? Turn to a partner, and try to come up with a few ways that our friend could control his wiggles.

MOVIE USHER
Ten more seconds...
Five more seconds...
Okey-dokey. We have many ideas to work with.

Can you try to hold on until the end of the movie?

MOVIE PATRON 1
I guess I can try being self-controlled. But *I'm* picking the movie next time.

MOVIE PATRON 2
OK. *Fine.* But I want to enjoy the rest of *this* movie.

(**Surprised and angry**) What? The movie is over. I missed the whole thing! I don't know how Sweet Susie Librarian caught the girl with the overdue book!

(**To Movie Patron 1**) Hey, do you remember that chase scene you wanted to see?

MOVIE PATRON 1
(**Nervously**) Uh, yeah. I gotta run...

Movie Usher turns to Movie Patron 1.

Movie Patron 1 hurriedly exits STAGE RIGHT.

Movie Patron 2 chases after Movie Patron 1 and exits.

Movie Usher chases after Movie Patron 2 and exits.

MOVIE PATRON 2
Come back here...come back here...

MOVIE USHER
(**Calling offstage**) This would be a good time for some self-control of your own!!

FOR DEEPER LEARNING

SAY: *We all get the wiggles from time to time. Some kids just seem to* always *have the wiggles; they're just wired that way.*

The advice the Usher gave is fine, and it's helpful. But there's someone else who can help you with the wiggles when they take over too: God. Second Timothy 1:7 says that God gives us a spirit of self-control. Self-control means deciding to not distract others even if sitting still is hard. Maybe a time to ask God for help with controlling the wiggles would be during church or during a test at school. Ask:

- *Have you ever met a kid who just seems to never be able to sit still? What is it like to be around someone like that?*

- *How can you help someone who has a case of the wiggles?*

- *Why is it important to let your parents or teachers know if you struggle with the wiggles?*

- *How can God help you when you struggle with the wiggles?*

Test Anxiety

School Pressures: *Philippians 4:6-7*

Cast:

NORTON: himself

MALLORY: a bright, conscientious student who carries around test anxieties

SCOTT: a good student who is worried about pleasing his parents

LIBRARIAN: an industrial-strength librarian, eager to meet kids' needs

Costuming: All characters wear street clothes.

Props: Tape, index cards, and a large sign that reads "Library"

Setup: Before class, cut an index card in half, and tape a piece of card to one of Mallory's and Scott's hands to represent homework papers. Hang the sign that reads "Library."

SCRIPT

ACTIONS	WORDS
Play track 5 on CD A.	
Norton enters and moves to STAGE LEFT.	**NORTON** (**Addressing children**) Hey kids! Our acting troupe is about to come out and do a skit about school pressures. Do you ever struggle with your schoolwork? Turn to a friend in arm's reach, and share with him or her which subject in school is hardest for you. When the school bell rings, it's time for the skit to begin.
Mallory and Scott enter STAGE RIGHT and move to CENTER STAGE. Norton exits STAGE LEFT.	

MALLORY

Thank *goodness*, it's library time. I need time to study for my tests.

SCOTT

(**A little anxious**) *I* have to get ready for my test *and* write a four-page paper on the history of puppets. *Four* pages. Who does my teacher think I am—a machine?

Librarian enters STAGE LEFT.

LIBRARIAN

(**Uses a deep, burly voice.**) Speaking of machines, I have a shipment of study books for Mallory. Is there a *Mallory* here?

Scott and Mallory turn their heads toward the Librarian.

MALLORY

(**Uneasy**) I'm Mallory. What's all this? *I* didn't order any books.

LIBRARIAN

You'll need this shipment of books in order to be ready for your test. I'll be right back.

Librarian rushes and exits STAGE LEFT.

SCOTT

What did he mean by "speaking of machines"?

Oh, my…Mallory, do you see this? (**Pauses.**) The librarian is riding a forklift—*in the library*. (**Pauses.**) He must be bringing you two tons of books.

Scott and Mallory turn their heads to STAGE LEFT. They stare with their mouths hanging open. They startle when they hear the thump.

MALLORY

(**Shaken**) There must be some *mistake*. I'll *never* be able to read all these books in time for my tests.

Mallory moves STAGE LEFT and looks OFFSTAGE.

LIBRARIAN

(**From offstage, calling**) No mistake, ma'am. You have fifty pounds of spelling books, ninety pounds of reading books. Then there are the math and geography books. Better start reading.

Mallory turns and moves to CENTER STAGE.

MALLORY

(**Stammering**) I…I…I'll never be able to get through all those books. And I'm no *good* at taking tests. I get so nervous. I know the stuff, but I can never remember the right answers during the test. This is *awful.*

SCOTT

Well I'm glad I don't have *your* teacher. I thought *I* had it bad with this paper.

(**Dumbfounded**) Oh, dear. (**Pauses.**) I hope this isn't for me. (**Weakly**) *Mommy!*

Librarian enters STAGE LEFT. Scott crosses and stands next to Librarian.

LIBRARIAN

(**Proudly**) You thought I forgot you! There's everything you need to write that paper and get ready for the science fair experiment. (**Pauses.**) Gotta go.

Librarian exits STAGE LEFT.

Scott turns left and right throughout his part and becomes increasingly animated. He paces back and forth, wildly.

SCOTT

(**Puzzled**) Science fair experiment? (**Gasps, becoming increasingly panicked.**) I forgot the science fair experiment. *Oh no!* It's due tomorrow! My paper is due too. My dad is out of town. He won't be able to help me. (**Gasp**) My parents! Mom and Dad will be so disappointed if I don't get an A.

MALLORY

(**Concerned**) Are you all right? You don't look good.

Scott freezes in place with his mouth open. He's absolutely still…

SCOTT

(**Melodramatically**) The room is closing in. Can't breathe…

Librarian enters STAGE LEFT and looks toward Mallory and Scott.

MALLORY

(**Worried**) Scott. *Scott.* (**Shouting**) *Scott,* why don't you move? What's wrong with you?

Mallory turns her head, sees the Librarian, and rushes to his side.

Librarian moves to Scott and looks him over. Librarian turns and faces Mallory.

MALLORY
(**Frantic**) What happened to Scott? Why isn't he moving?

LIBRARIAN
(**To himself**) Hmmm. Interesting...textbook case.

Mallory, your friend has frozen up due to high levels of anxiety. He's so worried about his paper that he's frozen stiff. I've read about this.

MALLORY
What did the book say? What's the cure?

LIBRARIAN
(**Embarrassed**) I don't remember. You see, the book was due before I got to that chapter. I had to return the book so it wasn't overdue. No librarian worth his salt would turn in a book late!

I'll have to find that book and look up the cure.

Librarian hurriedly exits STAGE LEFT.

Mallory turns to Scott and moves to his side.

Mallory turns and addresses the audience.

MALLORY
This is awful. Poor Scott is so worried about school that he's frozen with anxiety. He's wasting precious study time.

Kids, maybe you can help. Have you ever been worried about having to take a big test? Or maybe you've worried about disappointing your parents if you didn't do well.

Turn to a partner, and talk about ways that you deal with school pressure. I'll wait.

Ten seconds.
Five seconds.
Wow. These are some good ideas.

Scott starts to move and look around.

SCOTT
(Confused) What happened? Where am I? I had this terrible dream! There was this forklift…and books…*lots* of books!

MALLORY
It wasn't a dream. You were so nervous about your paper that you froze stiff.

SCOTT
Then I heard the kids' ideas about dealing with school stress. I calmed down enough to move again…But I *still* have my paper and my science project due tomorrow.

MALLORY
And I have my tests…

Librarian enters STAGE LEFT.

LIBRARIAN
(Excited)…and I found the answer. The cure for school paralysis is…hey! Scott's moving! That's great. *How* did you do that? Did someone else help you?

MALLORY
(Interrupting) Saved by the bell. We'll have to pick this up later. Er, thanks for all your help.

Mallory and Scott exit STAGE LEFT.

LIBRARIAN
No problem! I'll be ready for you with my forklift! Good night!

Librarian calls after the children and then exits STAGE RIGHT.

FOR DEEPER LEARNING

SAY: *You know, the Bible has another solution for dealing with school pressure, or anything else that makes us worried.* Read Philippians 4:6-7.

Have children form groups of three or four and discuss:

- *How often do you feel school pressure? Why?*

- *Why do you think adults make such a big deal about grades?*

- *Why do you think it's important to pray when you are worried about school?*

SKIT FIVE:
TEST ANXIETY

Operation Stopwatch

Being Too Busy: *Psalm 131*

Cast:

JACK: a fun loving fellow just looking for a moment to play

COURIER: a mysterious "cloak-and-dagger" type messenger

MYSTERIOUS VOICE: an elusive spy master

Costuming:
Jack wears a T-shirt, a ball cap, and sunglasses. The Courier wears a white shirt, dark clip-on tie, and a fedora.

Props: Cassette tape

Setup:
Before the skit begins, use a rubber band to secure the cassette tape to the Courier's hand.

SCRIPT

ACTIONS	WORDS
PLAY TRACK 6 ON CD A.	
Jack enters from STAGE RIGHT and moves to CENTER STAGE.	**JACK** (**Satisfied**) *There* are my sunglasses! I thought I lost them. I've been so busy this week that I haven't played with my friends all week. I'm off to play "Super Spy Agent" with my friends at the playground. I just need to find my walkie-talkies…
Jack turns his head left and right.	Where did I put them?
Jack moves to STAGE LEFT.	(**Surprised**) Who could that be? (**Pauses.**) Come in.

Courier enters STAGE LEFT.

COURIER

(In serious '50s movie G-man voice) I have a super-secret package for Agent Jack. Are *you* Agent Jack?

JACK

(Confused) What? I…I'm about to *pretend* to be an agent. **(Suspicious)** Who are you?

COURIER

That's strictly need-to-know information. I'm going to play this tape. Listen closely. I'm only going to play it once.

Courier holds up cassette tape.

MYSTERIOUS VOICE

(Urgently) Agent Jack, this is *your* mission. Your room needs to be cleaned *before* you can go outside and play. This message will self-destruct in three minutes!

JACK

(Alarmed) A self-destructing message. I've seen those on TV shows. If I don't get my room cleaned…Ka-bloom! The whole place will explode. I *really* want to play, but a mission is a mission.

Jack hurriedly exits STAGE RIGHT.

COURIER

(To kids) Have you ever wanted to play but had to spend time doing chores? Turn to a friend, and tell that person what chores keep you from your mission of having fun. Remember, just the facts.

Ten seconds…
Five seconds…
That's some good stuff, agents.

Jack rushes in STAGE RIGHT and moves to CENTER STAGE.

JACK

(Out of breath) Mission accomplished! Now I get to go play?

Courier looks left and right, scanning for danger and then exits STAGE LEFT.

Jack turns and calls offstage after Courier.

Jack begins to move STAGE LEFT.

Courier enters STAGE LEFT.

Courier holds up tape as voice plays.

Jack runs off STAGE RIGHT.

Courier looks left and right.

COURIER
Great work, Agent! Commence with playing.

(**Calling**) I'm not really an agent, you know.

All right, it's time to play!

JACK
Someone at the door *again*? (**Calling**) Who is it?

COURIER
(**Disapprovingly, but even-toned**) I told you my identity is top secret information. You have another mission. I'll play the tape.

MYSTERIOUS VOICE
Headquarters *likes* your work. You've earned another mission. You must write your history paper about Civil War yo-yos *before* you can go play. *This* message will self-destruct in three minutes.

JACK
(**Worried**) My history paper! I didn't know I had a history paper to write. I'm *never* going to get to go outside and play.

COURIER
(**To kids**) That's a tough break for Jack. Nothing gets in the way of free time like schoolwork. So, how much time would you say you spend on homework a day? Fifteen minutes? An hour? Grab a friend, and *whisper* this confidential piece of information to him or her. I'll be on the look out for spies while you whisper.

Ten seconds…
Five seconds…

Hurry! Someone's coming. It could be a spy.

JACK
(**Winded, gasping for air**) *Done!* Time to go play now.

COURIER
Roger that. Keep up the good work.

JACK
(**Takes a deep breath.**) OK. My hat. Where is my hat?

Four o' clock? This day is almost over! I hope my friends are still on the playground.

COURIER
I got past your security check post. Your security system needs improvement, Agent.

JACK
(**Impatient**) You *again*. I left the door unlocked. I was on my way out. I want to go have some *fun.*

COURIER
(**Maintaining even emotions**) There's nothing more fun than accomplishing a mission. *Nothing* at all. My mission is to deliver this tape to you. There's fun written all over my face. *See?*

Here's your mission…

MYSTERIOUS VOICE
You are doing a *great* job, Agent. Here's your mission: Practice your piano lesson, and get ready for the recital. This message will…

Jack enters from STAGE RIGHT and moves to CENTER STAGE.

Courier exits STAGE LEFT.

Courier enters STAGE LEFT.

Courier holds up tape.

JACK

(Interrupting)…I know. This message will self-destruct…

MYSTERIOUS VOICE

(Interrupting) No, this message won't blow up. Those self-destructing tapes are expensive. *This* tape will just get increasingly irritating by playing bagpipe music.

JACK

Bagpipes? **(Shudders)** Enough said. I'll start practicing.

Jack exits STAGE RIGHT.

(Disappointed) I'm never going to get to go play.

Courier looks left and right.

COURIER

(To kids) Lessons and practices: They gobble up your free time. Raise your hand if you take music lessons. **(Pauses.)** Raise your hand if you have sports practices. **(Pauses.)**

Raise your hand if you spend a lot of time at church. **(Pauses.)**

Raise your hand if you are in other clubs or activities.

Wow, you kids are busy. Looks like the case of the missing free time.

Jack enters STAGE RIGHT.

JACK

Done. You know, it's a funny thing. I was at the piano, and I realized a few things. My room *was* fairly clean. I don't *have* a history paper due. Most surprising, **(shouting)** I don't know *how* to play the piano.

COURIER

(Flustered) Well you did a *fine* job for a rookie. **(Pauses.)** This *is* 515 West Mapleburger Avenue?

JACK

No, this is 515 *East* Mapleburger Avenue.

COURIER

(Lights are coming on) You aren't a secret agent, *are* you?

JACK

I *tried* to tell you that.

COURIER

(Apologetically) Sorry about the confusion, sir. I'm going to have to ask you to tell *no one* what you've seen today. I have some work to do. There's an agent out there with *way too much* free time on his hands.

JACK

(Muttering) Un-be-lievable! I guess I have a little time to play before I have to go to Grandma's house for dinner at five o'clock

Oh, no! I've spent this whole day doing "missions." I ran out of time to play! I know this, tomorrow afternoon *my* mission is to do some serious playing.

Courier exits STAGE LEFT.

Jack begins to exit STAGE LEFT.

Jack exits STAGE LEFT.

FOR DEEPER LEARNING

SAY: **Boy it's easy to get so busy that you get all stirred up inside. But, God wants to help us not be stressed out over busyness.** Read Psalm 131.

Have children form groups of three or four and discuss:

- *What things make you too busy?*

- *When you get too busy, what kinds of things do you stop doing first? Why?*

- *How can being quiet with God help you deal with busy times?*

Commercial Break

Family Conflicts: *Ephesians 5:33*

Cast:

DIRECTOR NORTON: professional but nervous

SUE: a seasoned actor unhappy with her work conditions

EDWARD: a veteran thespian who wants the important roles

FRITZ: a young actor eager to make a splash

Costuming: All characters wear street clothes.

Props: None

SCRIPT

ACTIONS	WORDS
PLAY TRACK 7 ON CD A. Director Norton enters excitedly from STAGE LEFT. Sue, Edward, and Fritz enter from STAGE RIGHT and move to CENTER STAGE. Fritz looks around him. Sue turns to Director Norton and glares.	**DIRECTOR NORTON** Places, *places* everyone! It's time for us to produce our troupe's first ever TV commercial. This is *big* stuff, gang. Once people see this commercial, we'll be famous. We'll have acting jobs lined up from here to Timbuktu! **FRITZ** (**Awestruck**) A real live TV studio. Awesome. We've come a long way from performing at Joey Berkalipp's third-grade birthday party. **SUE** (**Uses rich English accent throughout.**) Humph. You think so? Joey at least had the good taste to provide his actors with *refreshments*. The candy dish in my dressing room was empty today.

Director Norton turns and faces the appropriate actor as he outlines their roles in the commercial.

Fritz nods his head, eagerly. Sue and Edward turn their heads away from Director Norton and huff.

Director Norton and Edward exit STAGE LEFT and STAGE RIGHT, respectively.

EDWARD
(Interrupting) Save it, sister. I've got real problems…I don't have enough lines in this script. The story isn't about *me*.

DIRECTOR NORTON
(Impatiently) The story is *about* Cowboy Carl's Family Burger Barn. Your job, Edward, is to play the part of the father. Susan, you play the mother. Fritz, you play the part of the happy son.

All of these other issues are going to need to wait until after we're done shooting this commercial.

(To children) I almost forgot. I need your help making this commercial. Whenever you hear me or any of the actors say *Cowboy Carl's Family Burger Barn*, I want you to holler (hollering) "Yee-haw!"

Let's try it: Cowboy Carl's Family Burger Barn. (Pauses.) *Very* nice.

OK, roll 'em. Cue the music.

FRITZ
(Eagerly, too hammy) Hey Mom, I'm *starving*. What's for dinner?

SUE
(Cheesy and without her accent) I don't know. I *burned* the deep-fried pizza. The refrigerator is *empty*, and it's time for dinner.

FRITZ
I know! When Dad gets home, we can all go to Cowboy Carl's Family Burger Barn. (Pauses.)

Edward storms back on stage from STAGE RIGHT.

EDWARD
This is an outrage! Do you see how *long* this commercial has gone without me having a *single* line? I deserve better treatment than this.

SUE
(**Breaking character and returning to accent**) Better treatment? You could have at least made sure that our (**punching each syllable**) *di-rect-or* had the common sense to feed us before we started acting. You *could* have asked him to order some takeout from Cowboy Carl's Family Burger Barn. (**Pauses.**)

EDWARD
That's *my* fault? Puh-lease! But, I see where you could work up an appetite—it's because you have to say all the *good* lines.

Fritz looks around as if worried.

FRITZ
(**Worried**) This isn't in the script. We're supposed to be a happy family on the way to Cowboy Carl's Family Burger Barn. (**Pauses.**) You kids are good.

Director Norton enters STAGE LEFT. Director Norton stomps as he lectures.

DIRECTOR NORTON
(**Aghast**) What's going on? Why all the bickering? You need to be a *happy* family if we are going to sell food from Cowboy Carl's Family Burger Barn. (**Pauses.**)

Sue sharply turns her head away from Edward.

SUE
My *"husband"* only thinks about himself.

Edward sharply turns his head away from Sue.

EDWARD
My *"wife"* won't let me get a word in. Seriously, this script isn't working for me.

Fritz moves far STAGE RIGHT and looks away from Sue and Edward.

FRITZ
(**Angry**) My *"parents"* stink! All they do is fight.

DIRECTOR NORTON

(**Commandingly**) *Enough!* We need to focus. This family *will* stay together long enough for me to film this commercial.

From the top…

Director Norton exits STAGE LEFT. Edward follows, sulking.

FRITZ

(**Eagerly, too big**) Hey Mom, I'm *starving.* What's for dinner?

SUE

(**Cheesy**) I don't know. I burned the deep-fried pizza. The refrigerator is empty, and it's time for dinner. We should go to Cowboy Carl's Family Burger Barn. (**Pauses.**)

Edward storms in from STAGE LEFT.

EDWARD

(**Incredulous**) How *dare* you? You…you intentionally stole my line!

SUE

(**Defensive**) I did not. I'm hungry. We really *should* go to Cowboy Carl's Family Burger Barn. (**Pauses.**)

SUE AND EDWARD

(**To children**) Stop that! We're having a family fight.

FRITZ

(**Melodramatically**) What about the love? Why can't we get along? (**To children**) This is just like my *real* family. My parents are always fighting. I hate it.

Director Norton enters from STAGE LEFT.

DIRECTOR NORTON

No, no, no! This is all wrong. Why can't you be a happy family—even for a few hours?

SKIT SEVEN:
Commercial Break

SUE
Have you ever tried to be pleasant on an empty stomach?

EDWARD
Or had to work with someone who steals *your* part?

DIRECTOR NORTON
(**Fuming**) Tha-at's it! We're taking a break for an hour. We're going for a drive. This TV family is *going* to work this out. We are *going* to be famous, or at least be able to pay the rent this month. Everyone, *march* to my car and no complaining.

Sue and Edward exit STAGE LEFT.

FRITZ
Where are we going? What's your plan to save our family?

DIRECTOR NORTON
I don't have a plan yet. I'm still working on that. I *do* know where I'm taking everyone. We're going to sit down for lunch, and we aren't getting up until we have things ironed out.

FRITZ
Great idea. Where are we going to eat?

DIRECTOR NORTON
Where else? Cowboy Carl's Family Burger Barn. (**Pauses.**)

BOTH Director Norton and Fritz exit STAGE LEFT.

Teacher Tip

Are there children in your class who have been touched by divorce? Remember these important points.

- Children often assume that they are somehow to blame for the parents' conflict. You can help assure the child that he or she isn't to blame.

- Kids need to know that God loves their parents and can help them through any hard time.

FOR DEEPER LEARNING

SAY: *Wow! This TV family is having a hard time staying together.* Read Ephesians 5:33. *God wants husband and wives to love each other and stay together. Sometimes our parents fight, and those fights can get serious.*

Have children form groups of three or four and discuss:

- *Why do you think parents get into fights sometimes?*

- *How do you feel when your parents fight?*

- *How can being friends with God help you when you see Mom and Dad fighting?*

Canceled

A Parent's Unemployment: *Matthew 6:25*

Cast:

SUE: a levelheaded actor who has seen a lot both on and off stage

EDWARD: an actor who is just as melodramatic in the green room as he is on stage

FRITZ: an eager but somewhat oblivious worker

Costuming: All characters wear street clothes.

Props: A baseball cap and a large sign that reads "Dogs: A 'Ruff' Look at Man's Best Friend"

Setup: Hang the sign near the stage. Place the baseball cap onstage where kids won't see it.

SCRIPT

ACTIONS	WORDS
PLAY TRACK 8 ON CD A. Edward and Sue enter from STAGE LEFT and move CENTER STAGE. Edward turns to Sue.	**EDWARD** **(Dejectedly)** How *does* this happen? Our musical "Dogs" has been canceled after just three weeks! **SUE** The audiences *hated* our show…that's how.

EDWARD

How could people hate a musical about man's best friend—the dog?

I thought I played a *convincing* St. Bernard. **(Howling mournfully)** Ooooh!

FRITZ

(With a gung-ho demeanor) Don't mind me! I'm just here to get the stage ready for the next musical. This one didn't do so well. It was a really *"dog"* of a show. Get it? Dog of a show.

Wow, not a chuckle. Tough crowd.

SUE

(Struggling to be polite) We get it. Very *funny*. We were actors in "Dogs."

FRITZ

Oh, my bad. I didn't know. Too bad the audience didn't *throw you a bone*. Get it? Throw you a *bone*? **(Pauses two beats, resuming sheepishly.)** I'll be over here cleaning.

EDWARD

So what are we going to do? We have no money, and now we have no job.

SUE

I'm not sure. But the director is already out there looking for more work for us.

EDWARD

Looking for work...*looking for work*?! It could take *months* before we find another theater that will invite us to perform "Dogs." We...we could *starve* to death in the meantime!

Fritz enters from STAGE RIGHT.

Fritz exits STAGE LEFT.

SUE

We're going to have to be more careful with our money. You'll need to stop buying that expensive bottled water.

EDWARD

No more bottled water? But my *voice*, my golden voice. I need to treat it like the fine instrument it is…

SUE

…and no more buying that expensive dog food. I don't know what you do with that anyhow.

EDWARD

I eat that dog food to help me get into my character. Eating dog food helps me *understand* what it would be like to be a majestic St. Bernard.

SUE

And when you stop eating the dog food, you won't need to buy those expensive breath mints.

Fritz enters STAGE LEFT. Fritz tells his joke animatedly. Fritz throws his head back while laughing.

FRITZ

Ouch! Someone's in the doghouse for being a big spender. *Get* it? Doghouse? Big spender?…ha, ha…

(Noticing no one else is laughing, sheepish) I just came in to find out what I should be doing with that giant fire hydrant prop. I'll figure something out on my own.

Fritz exits STAGE LEFT.

EDWARD

(Dramatically) Woe is me! I am a great classical ac-*tor*. Now I am without a penny to my good name. I shall starve!

Sue steps closer to Edward to comfort him.

SUE

(**Assuring**) Come on, every dog has his day. Ours is coming.

EDWARD

It's a dog-eat-dog world. I'm *not* waiting for the director to find us work.

(**Suddenly purposeful**) I have an idea. No strike that. I have an inspiration.

(**To children**) Kids, we need your help. We have no money, we are out of work, and we are, in fact, penniless.

SUE

Penniless? What happened to last night's ticket money?

Edward hangs his head.

EDWARD

I spent it on dog food. How was I to know that we would be canceled?

Children, I am appealing to your sense of generosity. Please check your pockets now for loose change. No coins? No problem. We'll take lint, paper clips, or rubber bands. I'm sure that we can get *something* for all that at the recycling plant. Please check now. I'll wait. (**Hums to self.**)

Edward holds up the baseball cap so kids can put items in it.

Dum de dum de dum.

Five seconds…

Edward looks into the cap.

Hmmm. We've collected seventeen pieces of paper, a rock, a frog, a dirty tissue. This might not have been a good approach.

SUE

We *could* sell some of our things. Maybe we could sell some of our costumes to make money.

SKIT EIGHT:
Canceled

Fritz enters STAGE LEFT, listens, and nods his head.

EDWARD
Sell my costumes? I *love* my dog costume. Besides, what if I sell it and then "Dogs" becomes a big hit? I need to be able to work again.

FRITZ
You'll be working like a dog in no time flat. **(Changes to a more serious tone.)** All joking aside, it's scary not having a job and worrying about money. I was out of work recently. I have a wife and two kids. It was a *hard* time.

SUE
What did you do?

FRITZ
Money was tight for a while. It was hard on the kids. We didn't have money for fun stuff. The kids worried. But we prayed and I looked for work every day. Eventually I got this job, working as a stagehand.

Speaking of work, I need to lock up. I'll show you out. I'll pray you find work soon.

EDWARD
(Miserable) Thanks. All this talk about making sacrifices and tightening the belt is simply depressing.

Edward exits STAGE RIGHT.
Sue and Fritz move STAGE RIGHT. Sue turns to Fritz.

SUE
What kind of work did you do before you became a stagehand?

FRITZ
Well, believe it or not, I used to be a writer. I wrote musicals. In fact, the last musical I ever wrote...was "Dogs."

Fritz and Sue exit STAGE RIGHT.

FOR DEEPER LEARNING

Read Matthew 6:25-27. SAY: *Jesus said not to worry about food and clothing. He promises to meet our needs. But sometimes it's hard not to worry about these things, especially if your parents have ever lost their jobs.*

Have the children form groups of three or four. Ask:

- *Have you ever been worried about your family having enough money? What was it like?*

- *Do you remember a time when God took care of your family? How did it feel?*

- *What's the best part of knowing that God promises to take care of our needs?*

Candy Store

Responsibility: Colossians 3:23-24

Cast:

CHIEF CANDY MAKER: a serious but kind woman

ASSISTANT CANDY MAKER: a free spirit needing to learn responsibility

NORTON: only hear his voice offstage in a phone call

Costuming: All characters wear street clothes.

Props: Licorice rope (one per child), toy phone, and a large sign that reads "Louie's Loopy Licorice Factory"

Setup: Before the skit begins, give each child a piece of licorice rope. Ask them not to eat it until after the skit. Hang the sign near the stage. Place the toy phone where puppets can access it. If your puppet will not be able to pick up the phone, use a small box that could be a speakerphone and have the character pretend to push a button to answer the phone.

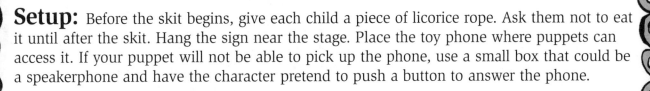

ACTIONS	WORDS
PLAY TRACK 9 ON CD A. Chief Candy Maker and Assistant Candy Maker enter from STAGE LEFT and move to CENTER STAGE.	**CHIEF CANDY MAKER** Are you *sure* that you're ready to handle the store alone? It's a *big* responsibility. **ASSISTANT CANDY MAKER** Of *course*! I won't let you down. I know how to run the licorice machine. I learned from the best!

CHIEF CANDY MAKER

(Flattered) You did, didn't you? (Thinking) OK, I'll let you run the shop for an hour. But, you need to be *working*. Don't think this is playtime! Watch the machines, and study for your candy maker's exams.

ASSISTANT CANDY MAKER

I know, I know. Go...have some fun. I'll take care of *everything*.

Assistant Candy Maker nods his head while Chief Candy Maker exits STAGE LEFT.

Ah, first phone call. I'll sell a billion miles of licorice.

Assistant Candy Maker answers the phone.

Hello, Louie's Loopy Licorice Factory. Can I help you?

NORTON

Hey, you've *got* to see what is on TV. There's a new superhero cartoon! Everyone is talking about it.

ASSISTANT CANDY MAKER

Assistant Candy Maker paces with excitement.

Cool! Oh, wait. (Disappointed) I *can't*. I'm watching the store all by myself, and I promised that I would be responsible.

NORTON

That's too bad. This is great. Gotta go. Commercial break is over.

ASSISTANT CANDY MAKER

Assistant Candy Maker hangs up the phone.

I *promised* I'd be responsible while the Chief Candy Maker was away: But a new superhero cartoon. This is tough.

Kids, have you ever had a tough time being responsible when there wasn't an adult to watch you? Maybe your parents are at work when you get home from school. Or maybe your mom wants you to clean your room without having to watch your every move.

Turn to a friend, and tell him or her ways you need to be responsible. I see you have a piece of our wonderful licorice. Each time you share something, tie a knot in your licorice rope. Can you be responsible and discuss this while I check on the licorice machines? I'll be right back.

(Hums to self while moving about as if working.)
Do..dee…doo de doo…
Do..dee…doo de doo…

Do you see your licorice ropes all tied up in a knot? *That's* how I feel right now. I *want* to make the Chief Candy Maker happy. But I *really* want to watch that cartoon. You know what? It wouldn't hurt if I watched a little bit of TV. Would it?

Turns to STAGE LEFT and acts as if switching on a television that's just offstage. Stays near STAGE LEFT while watching the offstage TV.

Ooooh…
Wow…
Awesome…

This is an amazing show! I *have* to find out if Bubble Gum Man can make it to Mean Mattie's hide-out by sticking to the bottom of his boots. But I need to get some work done too…hmmm.

Here's the plan. I'm going to turn up the dial on the machine to "high gear." The machine will make the licorice *twice* as fast. I'll watch my show and still make the candy in time. Then I'll study for my test during the commercials.

Assistant Candy Maker exits STAGE RIGHT.

Assistant Candy Maker returns from STAGE RIGHT and moves to CENTER STAGE.

(To kids) What? You've never been tempted to take a shortcut from being responsible? I'm sure you have. Grab that friend, and tell that person about the kinds of things that tempt *you* not to be responsible. I'll just watch my show while you chat.

Here we go…back to our show. (Pauses three beats, cheering.) Come on, Bubble Gum Man. You can do it!

Assistant Candy Maker stares STAGE LEFT.

What's that noise? Probably nothing. (Pauses.)

Wait, that doesn't sound good. It's the licorice machine.

Assistant Candy Maker turns to children.

It's falling apart! I put it in high gear. Oh, the Chief Candy Maker *told* me not to do that.

(Horrified) I'm in so much trouble! I broke the machine. It costs thousands of dollars. The licorice won't be ready on time. And I won't have time to study for my test.

(Dejected) I had better start cleaning up this mess before the Chief Candy Maker gets back. What *am* I going to tell the Chief Candy Maker?

Assistant Candy Maker exits STAGE RIGHT.

SKIT NINE:
Candy Store

FOR DEEPER LEARNING

Let children eat their licorice.

SAY: *Wow, the Assistant Candy Maker has a lot of trouble ahead of him. It's hard to be responsible when no one is watching you.* Read Colossians 3:23-24. *Paul says that we need to remember we should be doing everything to make God happy.*

Have children form groups of three or four and discuss:

- *How could the Assistant Candy Maker take responsibility for the mess he made? What should he do? What should he say?*

- *How does knowing that Jesus watches everything we do help us be responsible?*

The Rescue

Dealing With Differences: 1 Samuel 16:7

Cast:

CAFETERIA MAN: a superhero who put the *mystery* in mystery meat

SUPER GLUE: a superhero learning to control her powers of adhesion

NORTON: himself

CALVIN: a witty, self-confident person who is blind

Costuming:
Super Glue and Cafeteria Man both wear capes and T-shirts. Cafeteria Man wears a hair net. Norton and Calvin wear street clothing. Calvin wears sunglasses.

Props:
A dowel rod painted white

Setup:
Use tape to attach the dowel rod to one of Calvin's hands.

SCRIPT

ACTIONS	WORDS
PLAY TRACK 10 ON CD A. Norton enters, crosses to CENTER STAGE, and addresses children.	**NORTON** Hey kids! Glad you've joined us for another exciting episode of *Hall of Superheroes.* In today's episode, our superheroes are going to learn a lesson about the things that make us different from each other. I'm not talking about differences that we feel good about, like being stronger than other people, or being the smartest kid in your class. Our superheroes are going to be looking at the differences that make us feel uncomfortable and out of place.

Have you ever felt different from other people in a way that made you feel this way? Turn to a partner, and tell him or her about a time when you felt different from everyone else. I'll wait.

All right, that was some good sharing. I guess we all feel different and out of place from time to time. Let's see what happens with our show.

(**Surprised**) It's Super Glue and Cafeteria Man! Speaking of out of place, what are you two doing on stage? You aren't due on stage until page 7 of the script.

Cafeteria Man and Super Glue enter from STAGE LEFT. Norton turns his head and notices the superheroes.

CAFETERIA MAN
(**Discouraged**) We're having a slow day. No one wants to be rescued, at least by *us*.

SUPER GLUE
Look at us. Who wants to be rescued by a woman whose superpower is sticking to anything she touches?

CAFETERIA MAN
Or who wants to be rescued by a hero whose superpower is planning school lunchroom menus? *We're just too different to be heroes.* (**Sighs.**)

Norton takes a step away uneasily from Super Glue.

That is, unless *you* need rescuing. Norton, do you have a sliver that needs to be pulled? Or maybe a cat stuck in a tree?

NORTON
(**Uneasy**) No. No. I'm *fine*. Um, I've never felt better. In fact, I think I'll be going now!

Norton exits STAGE LEFT.

Calvin enters STAGE RIGHT. Super Glue leans into Cafeteria Man.

SUPER GLUE
(**Softly**) Do you see that, man? He's blind.

CAFETERIA MAN
(**Softly**) How can you *tell*?

SKIT TEN:
The Rescue

Super Glue and Cafeteria Man move next to Calvin.

SUPER GLUE

(Softly) He's wearing glasses, and he's carrying around a white cane. He's *different*. He must need our help. Let's go!

(In an energetic superhero voice) Sir, we see that you *cannot* see. We are *superheroes*, here to rescue you!

CALVIN

(Confused) Superheroes? Rescue…what do I need to be rescued from?

Calvin looks around as if puzzled by their offer.

CAFETERIA MAN

You're a brave, brave man. You need rescuing from everyone who makes fun of you because you are blind.

Cafeteria Man steps closer to Calvin.

CALVIN

Makes *fun* of me?! No one is making *fun* of me. (Irritated) I mean, every once in a while I come across a mean person who thinks it's funny. But I *don't* need to be rescued.

SUPER GLUE

(Puzzled) No one makes fun of you because you are different? *I* get picked on all of the time. Last week I accidentally got stuck to a mailbox. Everyone *laughed* at me. I felt like a fool.

CAFETERIA MAN

The children at the school tease me and say that meals I serve could *kill* someone.

I am so *misunderstood*. (Sighs.) My superpowers make me an outcast.

CALVIN

(Suspiciously) You want to rescue me because no one else will let you? You think that because I'm different, that I need your help?

CAFETERIA MAN

Absolutely. Surely you need help crossing the street?

CALVIN

I have a Seeing Eye dog for when I go walking around town. Check this out. **(Calling)** Marshmallow? *Marshmallow! Speak!*

CALVIN

Pretty cool, huh? So *no*, I don't need to be rescued.

SUPER GLUE

(Eagerly) Well then, maybe you need someone to keep you company. I bet being different keeps you from having enough friends.

CALVIN

(A little indignant) I have a *lot* of good friends. But, I'm beginning to wonder if *you* are doing OK in the friendship department.

SUPER GLUE

(Becoming emotional) People are afraid to get too close to me. They might end up being stuck to a tree. It's *lonely* being different.

Super Glue turns to speak to the audience.

Kids, how do you feel when other people focus on the thing that makes you different? Quietly turn to a partner, and make a face that tells how you feel when you think everyone is staring at you.

(Pause three beats) That's what I thought. **(Crying)** I don't *like* being different!

CALVIN

(**Understandingly**) Hey, don't cry. I *hate* it when superheroes cry. Look, I can't go skateboarding or play football, so I *do* feel left out sometimes.

But, I'm *cool* with being different. I'm the only person I know who can read with my hands. I also can't judge people by the way they look or dress. I have to choose my friends by trying to figure out what they're like on the inside.

CAFETERIA MAN

Really? (**Hopeful**) So, let's *pretend* that one of the side effects of my superpowers was that my sweat was like five-day-old grease. That wouldn't bother you?

CALVIN

I can't...I mean I *wouldn't* be able to see the hypothetical grease stains on your armpits.

You two need to focus on how your differences make you special.

CAFETERIA MAN

Hmmm. (**Confidently**) I *can* whip up a mean pudding using any available leftovers.

SUPER GLUE

(**With growing pride**) I *did* make that bank robber stick to the wall until the police arrived. Not everyone can do that.

CALVIN

(**Teasing**) If you two work together, you can make a meal that sticks to the roof of your mouth.

Marshmallow? Marshmallow!

Calvin turns and looks STAGE RIGHT.

Cafeteria Man and Super Glue hurriedly exit STAGE RIGHT.

CAFETERIA MAN
Marshmallow chased a cat up a tree. Now he can't get down. We're on it! We'll save your dog. Let's *go* Super Glue. We get to rescue someone!

CALVIN
(**Worried**) Wait for me. I'm coming. I hope you two know what you are doing. *Marshmallow, be careful!*

Calvin exits STAGE RIGHT.

FOR DEEPER LEARNING

SAY: *Sometimes it is hard to be different from other people. Sometimes people make fun of others because they have different cultures, or skin color, or disabilities. But to God, these differences aren't a problem.* Read 1 Samuel 16:7.

Have children form groups of three or four and discuss:

- *How is the way that Calvin evaluates people like how God sees people?*

- *Why do you think people make fun of the differences in others? How do you think God feels about this?*

- *How can God use the ways you are different to do special things?*

Scene From an Amusement Park

Fear of Abandonment: *Joshua 1:5b*

Cast:

   EDGAR: an overly dramatic and anxious amusement park patron

   WOMAN: a tourist wanting to relax and watch people

   MAN: a type A vacationer with a strong need to take in the whole park

Costuming: All characters wear present day street clothes.

Props: A sign that reads "The Really Big Amusement Park"

Setup: Hang the sign near the stage.

SCRIPT

ACTIONS	WORDS
PLAY TRACK 1 ON CD B. Edgar enters from STAGE RIGHT and hurriedly moves to CENTER STAGE. Edgar looks left and right, worried.	**EDGAR** This is terrible. Simply terrible. My friends and I agreed that if we lost each other at the park, that we would meet at the Ferris wheel. Well we lost each other in that big crowd. I can't find my friends anywhere. This is terrible. **(Pauses two beats.)** Where could they be?

Edgar steps forward and looks at the children. Edgar moves DOWNSTAGE as he talks, looking around.

(Noticing the children) You look like trustworthy people. Have *you* seen my friends? You'd know them if you saw them. Ivan is somewhat tall, and he has *really* bad breath. He ate seven hot dogs before getting on the roller coaster. He threw up coming down the first hill. Pee-hew, talk about bad breath.

Have you seen him? Or my friend Molly?

I'm alone. **(Dramatically)** I've been *abandoned* in this great, *big*, scary amusement park.

WOMAN
(Delighted) Isn't this a fantastic day? All the people, the food…

Woman and Man enter STAGE LEFT, crossing to STAGE RIGHT, talking to each other the whole time.

MAN
(Overly serious) *Focus!* We've got three hours left before the park closes. My chart says that we have ten more rides left to ride. The average length of a line is forty minutes. We are never going to finish the park. We need to *focus!*

WOMAN
Relax! This is supposed to be fun. Let's take in all the sights, the people…

EDGAR
(Tentatively) Excuse me. I need your help. I have a small problem—**(Suddenly, very melodramatic)** I'm lost in this big amusement park. And my friends have *abandoned* me. They aren't coming back. Ivan and Molly should be looking for me. They're probably riding rides and having fun.

Can you help me find my friends?

Skit Eleven:
Scene From an Amusement Park

WOMAN
(**Warmly**) Why certainly, we can help...

MAN
(**Guarded**) No, we *can't*. We have to get to the Atomic Polka Machine. It's the best ride in the park, and we haven't been on it.

Look, buddy, you'll find your friends. But, we have to go...

EDGAR
(**Increasingly worried**) But...but...I'm alone. I only have $5, and amusement park food is so overpriced. I'm going to starve! Look, there's some cotton candy on the ground. And there's half of a bacon burger! Maybe I could live for a few days by eating whatever I find on the ground.

(**Breaking into tears**) I'm alone in the world. I'll *never* see my friends again. *Never*...(**Now wailing**) Never...

(**Suddenly composed, gathering himself**) I...I don't need them. I don't need anyone—especially *not* Ivan and Molly. I'll die an old man in this amusement park. An old, abandoned, lonely man. (**Sobbing**)

(**Desperate**) *You!* You *have* to help me. Take me in. I'm an orphan. Adopt me. I'll be the son you never had. I'll mow the lawn seven times a day. I'll never complain when you cook bratwurst and liver omelets.

MAN
(**Annoyed**) Look. I don't *know* you. You're making me nervous. Back off!

Man and Woman exit STAGE RIGHT. Woman looks over her shoulder at Edgar as they exit.

Edgar bends over.

Edgar stands and waves his arms dramatically.

Man and Woman enter STAGE RIGHT. Edgar turns and notices them and lunges toward them. Both Man and Woman step back with a start.

EDGAR

But I'm *lost*. My friends and I agreed that if any one of us got lost, that we'd meet at the Ferris wheel. My friends have forgotten poor, lost Edgar.

WOMAN

This isn't the *Ferris* wheel. You're standing in front of the *ferret's* wheel. That's a completely different ride. We're on our way to the Ferris wheel. You can come with us.

MAN

He can? Are you sure about this? He looks dangerous…

EDGAR

(**Passionately**) Thank you, thank you so much. My life is saved! You *saved* me…

Wait up!

Woman and Man exit STAGE LEFT.

Edgar chases after them.

FOR DEEPER LEARNING

SAY: *Wow, Edgar was really worried when he thought his friends abandoned him in the park. Have you ever felt you were abandoned?*

Have children form groups of three or four and discuss:

- *Have you ever been lost? How did you feel?*

- *Have you ever worried that your parents wouldn't be there for you anymore?*

SAY: *We know that our parents love us, but sometimes we worry that they might not be there for us. But we know that God loves us and is always there for us.* Read Joshua 1:5b.

- *How do you feel knowing that God will never leave you?*

SKIT ELEVEN:
Scene From an Amusement Park

Emergency Meeting of the Tree Frog Club

New School and New Friends: *Joshua 1:9b*

Cast:

PAULO: the president of the "Tree Frog Club" with more control over parliamentary procedure than his emotions

KIPP: the levelheaded one in the bunch

RICO: an adventure seeker

MOLLY: a vivacious newcomer

Costuming: All characters wear street clothes and ball caps.

Props: A folded piece of paper and a large sign that reads "Tree Frog Club: MEMBERS ONLY"

Setup: Hang the sign on the front of the stage. Fasten the paper to one of Paulo's hands.

SCRIPT

ACTIONS	WORDS
PLAY TRACK 2 ON CD B. Paulo enters STAGE RIGHT as if coming up steps.	**PAULO** (**Puffing, calling offstage**) I *told* you that we shouldn't have built our treehouse in such a tall tree. (**Panting**) The air is so thin. My heart is going to explode! I wanted to build the treehouse in that cute little tree on the corner.
Kipp and Rico both enter STAGE RIGHT, also using an exaggerated step technique.	**KIPP** (**Sarcastically**) That was a shrub, Paulo. We can't meet in a "shrub-house."

RICO

You'd look pretty silly playing "Tarzan" in a shrub that's only three-feet high.

PAULO

Be that as it may, I've called this emergency meeting of the Tree Frog Club together to make an important announcement. Rico, Kipp, it's time to come to order.

RICO

(**Excited**) Is it time to paint the treehouse?

PAULO

(**Admonishingly**) You know the official Tree Frog Club Rules. First the secret handshake. (**To children**) Hey, you tadpoles out there. Don't think I don't see you. You need to turn to a nearby friend and make up a secret handshake. I'll wait and sing the official Tree Frog Club Anthem while you make up your secret handshakes.

(Sings "Yankee Doodle" only using the word froggie for all the words.)

KIPP

(**Impatient**) OK, Paulo. We've done the anthem and the secret handshake. The meeting has officially come to order. What's the big announcement?

PAULO

I can't be president of the Tree Frogs any more. I'm moving to the other side of town.

KIPP AND RICO

(**Shocked**) You're *what*!?!

PAULO

(**Animated**) I'm moving next week. Oh, this is *awful*. I have to leave all my good friends. I won't see you guys as much.

KIPP

(**Still shocked**) Wow, I don't know what to say. I'm going to miss you.

RICO

Me too. Does this mean that *I* can be president now?

KIPP

(**Stern**) This is hardly the time Rico! (**To Paulo**) Have you seen your new school?

PAULO

Yeah. It's huge! There are hundreds of kids…and I don't know *one* of them. I have a hard time making new friends. What if I don't fit in? What if the other kids don't need a new friend?

MOLLY

(**In a thick southern accent, throughout**) Hey, y'all. Can I join you? Ma' name's Molly.

KIPP

Who's that?

MOLLY

Y'all know it's nawt ni-ice to whispa in front of a lady?

PAULO

(**Clearing his throat**) Excuse me, *Molly* is it? You are interrupting a super secret meeting of the Tree Frog Club. We're discussing sensitive matters…

RICO

(**Interrupting**)…like Paulo having to move away. He has to go to a new school and make new friends! He's worried about starting over…

Molly enters STAGE RIGHT using an exaggerated step technique.

Kipp leans into Rico.

PAULO

Rico! She's not a Tree Frog. We can't talk with her about this. She doesn't know the handshake, or the song…

MOLLY

But Ay *do* know what it's like ta be the new kid in the neighba'hood. This is mah furst day in tawn. You'll *neva* guess where I'm from!

PAULO

The deep south?

MOLLY

My dad's in the Awmee. So I've had to move a lot. This is the fourth time in three yee-ahs.

PAULO

(**Astonished**) Four times in three years? How do you do it? I mean how can you stand having to make friends so many times?

MOLLY

It's tough sometimes. But, I just take a deep breath and jump in.

PAULO

(**Enthused**) Tips on how to make friends? You *have* to tell me.

Molly slowly moves toward STAGE RIGHT and begins a stairs "descent."

MOLLY

(**Teasingly**) I do-o-on't know…this bein' a supa' secret club and all. Memba's only…

Molly turns and ascends the stairs.

PAULO

(**Alarmed**) Wait! Don't go! I need help with making new friends. (**Clears throat and speaks authoritatively.**) As president of the Tree Frog Club, I call for a vote that Molly be declared an official member of the club. All in favor say "ribbit."

PAULO, RICO, AND KIPP
(Loudly, in unison) Ribbit!

PAULO
Well that settles it. Congratulations Molly, you are an official member of our club. (Too eagerly) Now you can tell me…I mean us…your friend-making secrets.

MOLLY
Nothing's settled yet, boys. Where I come from…a deal is settled ova' a bowl of ice cream. See y'all at the ice cream stand. Bye, now.

RICO
Ice cream? I move that this meeting be officially ended, adjourned, over, kaput! I'll be at the ice cream parlor with Molly.

KIPP
She's good. She's *real* good. What are you going to do? Are you going to let her get away with this?

PAULO
Yes, yes I am. I need some friend-making pointers. Like you said, she's *real* good. She could even be the next president of the Tree Frogs by the end of the week.

Molly turns and exits STAGE RIGHT, using an exaggerated "stairs" technique.

Rico rushes off STAGE RIGHT.

Kipp turns his head toward Paulo.

Paulo looks at Kipp.

Paulo exits STAGE RIGHT followed by Kipp.

FOR DEEPER LEARNING

SAY: *It's hard going to a new school or moving and having to make new friends. But God promises to be with you—wherever you go.* Read Joshua 1:9b.

Have children form groups of three or four and discuss:

- *What do you think would be the hardest thing about moving? Why?*

- *How would knowing that God was with you help you make new friends if you moved?*

- *What friend-making advice would you give Paulo?*

- *What can you do to make new people in your school, church, or neighborhood feel more welcome?*

SKIT TWELVE:
Emergency Meeting of the Tree Frog Club

Skating Party of One

Loneliness: Matthew 26:40

Cast:

ANTHONY: a skater who isn't fitting in

DJ DAZZLE: the perennial perky DJ (an offstage voice)

FRITZ: a skater with no lines

EDWARD: a skater with no lines

Costuming: All characters wear street clothes.

Props: A large sign that reads "Skate Palace"

Setup: Fasten the sign to the front of the stage.

SCRIPT

ACTIONS	*WORDS*
PLAY TRACK 3 ON CD B.	
Anthony enters from STAGE LEFT and moves to CENTER STAGE. Throughout the skit, all puppets move with a side-to-side skating motion.	**DJ DAZZLE** (**Offstage voice**) Those were the sounds of "The Cheesy Grins." I'm DJ Dazzle, and you're at the Ridgefield Elementary School Skating Party—skating (**punching each word**) *with all your friends*! Enjoy the party!
Anthony faces forward and looks around to his left and right.	**ANTHONY** (**Discouraged**) All my *friends*, humph! Where *are* they? Where are Ian and Jessie and Dewey? I'm here all by myself.
Fritz and Edward enter STAGE LEFT, cross in front of Anthony, and exit STAGE RIGHT. They occasionally spin and twirl.	Excuse me…pardon…(**Calling after they pass him**) Hey, have you seen a tall kid with dark curly hair and…

Anthony continues swaying left and right in place.

Fritz and Edward enter from STAGE RIGHT and cross behind Anthony, making several twirling and spinning motions, and exit STAGE LEFT.

Anthony continues to sway in place.

Anthony does the motions to the song with the children.

Anthony turns his head and looks STAGE LEFT. His mouth drops open in shock.

Anthony moves back and turns his head from left to right quickly.

(**Discouraged**)…never mind. It looks like I'm here *all* alone.

DJ DAZZLE

(**Energetically**) Hey, *hey*! I'm back with a dedication song. This one is for Rashida from her *best friend* Heather. The song— "Forever Friends."

ANTHONY

(**Downcast**) Man, everyone has a friend here but me. I must look really stupid being out here by myself.

There are all these people around me. But me, I'm here all by myself. I feel all alone.

DJ DAZZLE

All right! It's time for a skating party favorite. It's time for the "Hokey Chicken Song." *Everyone* needs to participate. Hey you, kids in the audience, stand up and do the motions as you hear them.

(**Singing to the tune of "Row, Row, Row Your Boat"**)
   Place your left arm in the circle
   Shake it all around
   Jump up and down where you stand
   Fall and touch the ground.

   Place your right arm in the circle
   Shake it up and down
   Spin around and touch your knees
   It's time to sit back down.

Now wasn't that fun? There's *nothing* like a skating party with friends.

ANTHONY

(**Mournfully**) Why does she keep rubbing in the fact that I'm *alone*?

Ah! Speed skaters. I've *got* to get out of the way.

Wow! That was close.

(**Becoming increasingly deflated**) I like to skate fast...with my friends...who aren't here.

(**Sighs.**) Two more hours left of this skating party. I *wish* I could go home now. I guess I'll go hang out in the snack bar and wait this out.

DJ DAZZLE
All right, it's time for a partners' skate. Everyone grab a friend and get out on the floor! Let's go.

Anthony slowly skates off STAGE LEFT.

FOR DEEPER LEARNING

SAY: *It's hard when you feel alone. Did you know that even Jesus felt alone? The night before Jesus died, he was up late praying. He wanted his friends to stay awake with him, but they all fell asleep. Jesus was left all alone to think about dying on the cross.*

Have children form groups of three or four and discuss:

- *Have you ever felt alone? What did you do with those feelings?*

- *What is the difference between being alone and feeling lonely?*

- *What can you do when you feel alone?*

- *How can you help others that are feeling lonely?*

Crowded House

Feeling Replaced by a Baby: *Genesis 21*

Cast:

EDWARD: a melodramatic actor who discovers a soft spot for kids

SUE: a seasoned actor who is never too busy for a baby

FRITZ: a young, budding actor with no time to slow down for a baby

OFFSTAGE VOICE

Costuming: All characters wear street clothes.

Props: A diaper, a shoe box, a powder blue gift wrapping bow, and a sign that reads "Louie's Car Wash and Community Theater: Home of the Puppet Players"

Setup: Place the bow on the box to create a crib, and place this on stage left. Fasten the sign to the front of the stage.

SCRIPT

ACTIONS	WORDS
PLAY TRACK 4 ON CD B.	**OFFSTAGE VOICE** **(In a thick Brooklyn accent)** All right, that's the last car. Louie's Car Wash is officially closed for lunch. We'll be back in an hour.
Sue and Edward enter from STAGE RIGHT.	**EDWARD** …and the Puppet Player Community Theater is now *open*. We've got a busy weekend of rehearsal ahead.
Sue walks to the crib STAGE LEFT and looks into the crib. Sue turns and looks at Edward.	**SUE** Aren't you forgetting something? We're baby-sitting Baby Cole this weekend.

Edward walks next to Sue, and they both peer into the crib.

Fritz enters STAGE RIGHT. Fritz turns his head and looks around.

Sue leans into Edward.

Edward becomes distracted by the baby and bends over the crib and quietly coos at the baby.

EDWARD
I *did* forget. **(Cooing)** Wittle babby, go-go-giggle-go. Uncle Eddie's with you this weekend. **(To Sue)** I also forgot how wonderful babies are. We might not get much *else* done this weekend.

FRITZ
Sorry I'm late. I had a hard time finding the new theater.

Are you sure this is a good place for a theater? I'm sure you got a good price on the rent, but look at all these brushes, hoses, and **(noticing the crib)** there's even a *baby*. What's a baby doing here?!

SUE
Fritz, meet Baby Cole. We're watching him this weekend…

FRITZ
(Interrupting) *This* weekend? Oh, no, no, *no*! We've got *plans* this weekend. Ed, you promised to teach me everything you know about acting…

SUE
(Under her breath) *That* can't take too long.

FRITZ
…and Sue, you promised to take me to the library this weekend.

SUE
Oh, I *did* promise you that. Fritz, I'm sorry. Your Aunt Petunia called at the last minute and needed us to watch the baby. I can take you on Monday.

FRITZ
Monday! That's not fair. **(Turning to Ed)** Well at least you can give me some acting lessons. **(Pauses two beats.)** Ed?

SKIT FOURTEEN:
Crowded House

EDWARD

(Still engrossed in the baby) Goo-goo, pooh-pooh? A da-da, goo…

FRITZ

(Irritated) Hel-*lo*! Earth to Ed…Earth to Ed.

EDWARD

(Stammering) What? Ah, acting lessons…right. **(Suddenly confident)** Fritz, you say you want acting lessons. All right kid-o, I'm going to teach you the hardest role that you will ever play!

FRITZ

(Excited) Really? What's that?

EDWARD

I'm going to teach you how to play the part of a proud uncle.

(Noticing the audience) Hey kids, I'll give you acting lessons too. If you master *this* role, why then, you could go places!

Fritz and Sue rock back and forth.

First, pretend to rock the baby in your arms. **(Pauses two beats.)**

Fritz and Sue lean over the crib.

It's time to feed the baby. Give your baby a bottle. **(Pauses two beats.)**

Fritz and Sue face each other. Sue moves close to Fritz. Fritz bounces up and down to look like Sue is burping Fritz.

Now, burp the baby. Pat him on the back *ge-e-ently*. Easy does it. **(Pauses two beats.)**

Fritz moves away from Sue and pouts.

Uh, oh! Baby's got a full diaper! Better change the baby's diaper. **(Pauses two beats.)**

That's great. You kids did a great job. Someday you'll make great uncles and aunts…I mean actors.

Sue steps toward Fritz.

Fritz storms off STAGE RIGHT.

Edward turns his head and watches Fritz exit.

Both Edward and Sue move to the crib, peer in, and start playing with the baby.

FRITZ

(**Disappointed**) These acting lessons *stink*. You just can't stop thinking about the baby. Admit it—you like the baby more than me!

SUE

(**Admonishingly**) That's not true. It's just that babies are helpless. They can't do anything for themselves. They need lots of our time and attention.

FRITZ

(**Angry**) *Fine!* I know when I'm not wanted.

EDWARD

Wow. Having this baby around sure is hard on Fritz.

SUE

I know. But it's only for a weekend. Fritz is going to have to be flexible.

EDWARD

I agree. But maybe I can sneak in an acting lesson later.

You know, it sure is nice having a baby around.

SUE

(**In baby talk**) Goo-bee-doo-bee-do! Aunt Susie loves you!

EDWARD

Did you hear that? He likes you! Let me try. (**In baby talk**) Loopy-loopy-gaa-gaa! Doo-dee-doo-dee-do!

(**In fake shock**) *Well.* I've never been talked to like that. (**Laughing**)

Fritz enters STAGE RIGHT with a diaper fastened over his head.	**FRITZ** (**Pretending to be a baby**) Goo, goo. Goo, goo.
Sue turns and faces Fritz.	**SUE** (**In disbelief**) What are you *doing*?! Take that diaper off your head. You look silly.
Edward looks up from the crib and turns and faces Fritz.	**FRITZ** (**Still dead panning**) Goo, goo. Ga, ga. I am a baby—the center of the universe. I am the *only* person that matters.
Sue crosses to CENTER STAGE.	**SUE** (**Disapprovingly**) *OK*. We get the point. You're disappointed that the weekend plans changed.
	EDWARD And you're feeling a little jealous over the baby. Look, I'm sorry that the plans changed but…You know what? We can sneak some quick acting lessons…
	FRITZ (**Hopeful**) You mean it? Real acting lessons that have *nothing* to do with babies? Really?
Edward and Fritz begin to exit STAGE RIGHT.	**EDWARD** I mean it. Let's go.
Both Edward and Fritz stop. Edward hurries to the crib and bends over it.	(**Apologetically**) I'm sorry. I *really* am.
Fritz moves STAGE RIGHT and turns to see if he is being noticed. Fritz exits.	**FRITZ** (**Weakly**) But, you promised…
	(**Disappointed**) Fine, I'll just go outside and play by myself.

SKIT FOURTEEN:
Crowded House

Sue and Edward look up.

Sue bends over the crib to pick up the baby.

Both Sue and Edward exit hurriedly STAGE RIGHT.

OFFSTAGE VOICE
All right, lunch is over. Time to get back to work. We're going to fire up this car wash in three minutes.

SUE
Time to go. I'll take the baby. You find Fritz and try and reason with him.

EDWARD
OK. I'll give it my best. But he's having a hard time handling this baby being around.

FOR DEEPER LEARNING

SAY: *Have you ever had to make room for a new baby in your house? It's not easy. There was a boy in the Bible named Ishmael. He had a baby brother born into his home. He had a hard time handling it. He was actually mean to the baby and got into all kinds of trouble. It's hard sharing Mom and Dad's time and love with a new baby.*

Have children form groups of three or four and discuss:

- *Has it ever seemed like your parents didn't have time for you anymore? How did you feel?*

- *What kind of advice would you give Fritz?*

- *If your parents had a new baby, what are some ways that you could be helpful? How do you think you would feel after being helpful?*

SKIT FOURTEEN:
Crowded House

Boo!

Fear of the Dark: Matthew 14:22-33

Cast:

ALEX: a dramatic boy with a wild imagination

DAN: a tough guy by day, deathly afraid of the dark by night

SETH: an adventuresome soul determined to pull an "all-nighter"

SUE: herself

Costuming: All characters wear pajamas or sweats.

Props: None

Setup: None

SCRIPT

ACTIONS	WORDS
PLAY TRACK 5 ON CD B.	
Sue enters STAGE RIGHT and moves to CENTER STAGE.	**SUE** Hello boys and girls. In a brief moment, this tent will be filled with some *real* men. I'm talking about *manly* men. These *brave* men have but one weakness…they are deathly afraid of the dark. Can you help us tell this story? It takes place in the woods. We need lots of scary sounds that you might hear in the woods at night. Whenever you hear the sound of an owl "hooting," can you make your scary sound? Let's try it.

Sue exits STAGE LEFT.

Alex, Seth, and Dan enter STAGE LEFT.

(Pauses for three beats.) Yep, those will do. That's some pretty scary stuff.

I gotta go. I hear the guys coming.

ALEX
(Happily, laughing) That was a *great* campfire!

SETH
(Excited) I *know*! The s'mores, the hot dogs…

Dan turns his head to Seth.

DAN
(Laughing) I can't *believe* you ate fifteen s'mores, Seth! You're going to be *sick* tonight.

SETH
I better not get sick. I'm going to stay up all night. I'm not going to sleep one second!

Alex crouches toward Seth.

ALEX
If you're awake, maybe you'll see *Big Toe*, **(in an ominous voice)** the mighty monster of the deep woods.

DAN
Um, Alex, don't you mean Big Foot?

Alex turns toward Dan.

ALEX
Weren't you listening to the campfire stories tonight, Dan? **(Dramatically)** A few years ago Big Foot lost his big toe in a bear trap while trying to get out of a rainstorm. A bolt of lightning zapped the bear trap and brought his severed big toe back to life! Now Big Toe hunts the woods at night looking for people he can gobble up!

SETH
(Nervous) Some of those campfire stories were pretty scary. It's a good thing that none of *us* are afraid of the dark.

SKIT FIFTEEN:
BOO!

All puppets jump and look startled.

ALEX
That's right. I'm not afraid of the dark…I'm not afraid of Big Toe.

ALL
(**Pauses.**) What was that?!

ALEX
(**Nervously**) What was *that*?

DAN
(**Unsure**) I don't know. It was probably just the wind.

Seth jumps at Alex. Alex startles away.

SETH
(**Teasing**) Boo! It's Big Toe! Arghhh! (**In a scary voice**) I'm Big Toe! I'm going to get you.

Look, *I'm* not going to sleep. I plan to stay up all night. You two cowards try to get some sleep. I'll keep watch.

Alex moves STAGE RIGHT. Dan moves STAGE LEFT. Both Alex and Dan recline their bodies over the edge of the puppet stage with their arms and head drooping over the front.

DAN
I could use some sleep. Good night, Alex. Good night, Seth.

Seth leans over the CENTER STAGE and slumps his head and arms over the front of the curtain.

SETH
(**Talking to himself**) I'm not afraid of any monsters. No-sir-ee! (**Pauses one beat.**) Boy, it's dark out. It's kind of creepy. (**Yawns.**) I'm getting kind of sleepy…

ALEX
What's that?

All puppets wake up, startled.

DAN
It sounded like a coyote or a grizzly bear. *You* were keeping watch, Seth. Did you see what it was?

Alex and Dan both return to their sleeping positions.

Seth stretches and returns to his sleeping position.

Alex wakes up, startled. Alex looks around.

Alex returns to his sleeping position.

Dan quickly sits up.

Alex and Seth jump up. Both Alex and Seth turn to Dan.

SETH
(**Defensive**) I…I was awake. At least most of the time. I didn't see what it was. You two go back to sleep. (**Yawns.**)

I'll keep guard….

I'll stay up all night… Nothing will get past me…(**Yawns.**)

(**Snoring loudly**)
Zzzzzzzzzzzzzz…ZZZZZZZZZZ…zzzzz zzzzzzzzzz

ALEX
What was that? I had this dream about Big Toe. He was coming this way with a horrible growl!

SETH
ZZZZZZZZzzzzzzzzzzzzzz…

ALEX
That figures…It was just Seth *snoring* again. Nothing to worry about. I'll go back to sleep.

DAN
(**Yelling**) No! No! *No-o-o-o-o*! He's coming to get me! Aaaah!!!

ALEX
(**Alarmed**) What's wrong, Dan?

SETH
Who's going to get you?

DAN
(**Panting**) I had this terrible dream. I was trapped in a cave, and Big Toe was coming to get me…

Seth jumps.

Alex begins to exit STAGE LEFT.

All puppets startle and group close
together.

SETH

(**Scolding**) This isn't going to work! You
two *have* to get over your fears. There's no
reason to be afraid of the dark, or bad
dreams, or noises…

Ba-a-a-h! What *was* that? (**Panicking**)
That's it. *We're* out of here. Pack your
bags right now…'cause we're going home.

ALEX

(**Upset**) I'm with Seth. It's time to get out
of here while we can. I bet Big Toe is the
one out there making all that racket!

DAN

Wait! We can't leave right now. Think,
man, think! It's dark outside of this tent
and (**becoming sheepish**)…er…I need to
confess something…er…I'm afraid of the
dark. Secondly, if Big Toe is out there, in
the dark, he'll have the advantage.

SETH

(**Knowingly**) That's right. Everyone
knows that monsters can see in the dark.
We'll never find our way out of these
woods in the dark. We're just going to
have to gut it out until morning.

SETH

It's Big Toe. (**Terrified**) He's coming to get
us. We're doomed. *Doomed* I tell you.

DAN

Look. This is ridiculous. I'm just a little
afraid of the dark. I've always been afraid
of the dark.

ALEX

And I have bad dreams from time to time.
I *definitely* don't want another bad dream
like I just had…

Alex turns and looks off STAGE LEFT.

Dan and Seth join Alex.

Dan, Seth, and Alex all hurriedly exit STAGE LEFT.

SETH

(**Trying to be brave**) OK. That settles it. We'll have to break for it. We're going home!

There's only one Big Toe out there, and there are three of us. He can only eat *one* of us. On the count of three, we're going to make a mad dash for the house.

ALEX

(**Becoming braver**) I see the kitchen light. I think we can do this! On the count of three, we're going to run as fast as we can to the house.

Are you ready? One…. Two…

ALL

(**Screaming**) It's Big Toe! Aaaaaaaaah!

FOR DEEPER LEARNING

SAY: *Wow. Those guys certainly were afraid. Bad dreams, monsters, fear of the dark—that's scary stuff!*

Have children form groups of three or four and discuss:

- *What's the scariest dream you've ever had? How did you feel?*

- *Have you ever been afraid of the dark? How did you handle it?*

Open your Bible to Matthew 14. SAY: *Did you know that Jesus' disciples had a scary night once?* Tell the story of how Jesus walked on water from Matthew 14:22-33 in your own words. Ask:

- *What scary things did the disciples hear?*

- *What scary things did the disciples see?*

- *How did knowing Jesus was with them help them?*

- *How can Jesus help you when you are afraid at night? When you have a bad dream?*

Playground Sports Central

Being Picked Last: *Romans 12:6-8*

Cast:

REPORTER: an enthusiastic television commentator

OLLIE: an awkward and insecure guy

MIA: the consummate athlete who can do it all

DONOVAN: a great athlete who has a motor that doesn't stop

Costuming: Ollie, Donovan, and Mia wear T-shirts. Reporter wears a white shirt, black tie, and sunglasses.

Props: *(Optional)* If you are using arm rods with your puppets, consider fastening a toy microphone to one of the Reporter's hands.

Setup: None

SCRIPT

ACTIONS	WORDS
PLAY TRACK 6 ON CD B.	
Reporter enters STAGE LEFT.	**REPORTER** **(Energetically)** Welcome to another edition of Playground Sports Central! I'm Jim Naseum, and I'm here at Grandview Elementary School covering today's draft for kickball. I'll be updating you on the picks as they happen.
Mia enters STAGE LEFT.	But first, we have Mia with us for an exclusive interview. Mia is the captain of the Blue Team. She's an amazing athlete. She holds the school home-run record. Kids in the studio audience, give a big round of applause for Mia! **(Pauses.)**

Ollie enters STAGE RIGHT and begins to stretch and jog in place. Ollie turns to Mia while jogging in place.

Mia exits STAGE LEFT.

Ollie calls after her.

Ollie turns to Reporter.

Donovan enters STAGE RIGHT. Donovan moves next to the Reporter.

REPORTER
(To Mia) Mia, what's your strategy for deciding who to pick to be on your kickball team?

MIA
That's easy, Jim. I've played ball with the other kids in my class for several years now. I know who will be able to contribute and help us win. I'll be picking *winners*, Jim, *winners.*

OLLIE
(Eagerly) Hey, Mia. I've been working on my game lately. I've been working out and practicing my kicks. Hope you pick me.

MIA
(Hesitating) Uhm…we'll see. There are a lot of kids out there. Let's see how it goes…

OLLIE
All right. But if you pick me, I won't let you down.

REPORTER
That was unexpected. You have to respect Ollie's spunk. He asked Mia to pick him for her team, only one day after he dropped four easy outs.

OLLIE
(Indignant) Hey, I only dropped three balls, and the sun was in my eyes.

REPORTER
I have with me, Donovan, team captain for the Red Team. Everyone knows Donovan as the strong kid in his class. Donovan, your muscles will help you on the field, but have you thought through your strategy as to what kids you'll be picking for your team today?

SKIT SIXTEEN:
Playground Sports Central

Donovan points to his head.

Ollie edges Reporter aside and stands next to Donovan.

DONOVAN
Yeah, that's simple. I'm going to pick the *popular* kids. I figure I can make friends by picking the cool kids early. Pretty smart, huh?

OLLIE
(**Too eager**) Hey Donovan, how are you doing? Remember, me, Ollie? You *can't* go wrong if you pick me. I've got the right stuff. Pick me and you're sure to win.

DONOVAN
(**Unsure**) Who are you? I've never seen you before.

OLLIE
(**Surprised**) What? I've sat next to you in school for the past three years (**struck with realization**), and you don't know who I am?

Reporter squeezes between Ollie and Donovan and pushes Ollie aside. Ollie moves to STAGE LEFT.

REPORTER
(**To Ollie**) Get your own show, kid.

All right, it's time for the captains to select today's teams for kickball. Kids, help me make this look like a big-time television show. Would you applaud wildly every time a team captain makes a pick? It will make the show more interesting for the viewers at home.

Let me hear you applaud. Go ahead.

Mia enters from STAGE RIGHT and stands beside the Reporter.

Ollie turns and looks at Mia. Ollie begins to wave wildly.

(**Pauses.**) Wow that's great. OK Mia, you have the first pick.

MIA
Hmm. The first pick is an important one. I pick Joshua. (**Pauses.**) He's as fast as lightning.

OLLIE
(Muttering to himself) *I'm* fast. Why didn't she pick me?

REPORTER
Folks in TV land: that was a strong pick by Mia. Just last week, Joshua escaped sudden doom by outrunning the school bully on the playground. He's a fast, fast kid.

Donovan, it's your pick. You're on the clock. Who's it going to be?

DONOVAN
(To Ollie) Hey kid, can you stop jumping? I'm trying to see who's available.

Thanks. I pick Nasha. (Pauses.) Everyone likes Nasha. Having her on my team is a big boost for my popularity.

REPORTER
(To audience) This was an interesting pick. Nasha is only an average kickball player. But she is *very* popular. This move will help Donovan fit in at school. Strong play, Donovan.

Mia, your pick.

OLLIE
(Whispering to himself) Pick me, pick me, pick *me.*

MIA
I pick Angel. (Pauses.) She's a dynamo on the kickball field.

DONOVAN
Well I pick Michael. (Pauses.) Maybe Michael will invite me to his birthday party next month.

Reporter turns to Donovan. Ollie begins to jump up and down wildly, waving his arms.

Donovan lifts his head and tries to look past Ollie.

Ollie stops jumping. He slouches and hangs his head.

Skit Sixteen:
Playground Sports Central

Ollie steps forward to FRONT LEFT.	**OLLIE** (**Frustrated**) It doesn't matter what sport it is: kickball, dodge ball, or tiddlywinks. I'm always the last one picked. **REPORTER** Mia, your pick.
Mia places her hand on her chin. Ollie halfheartedly waves his hand. Reporter moves CENTER STAGE and faces forward.	**MIA** OK. I pick Brad. (**Pauses.**) **REPORTER** (**To audience**) Mia's team is filling up nicely. She's going to be fielding a contender today. Donovan is now on the clock. Your pick, Donovan.
Ollie sighs and hangs his head.	**DONOVAN** OK. I pick Spike. (**Pauses.**) Spike has a cool video game system. I'll be playing "Space Monkeys" for sure this weekend! **REPORTER** The tension is getting high for Ollie. Ollie holds the school record for being the last one picked. There are only two picks left. Ollie has only one chance left to *not* be the last one picked.
Ollie perks up, turns to Mia, and joins his hands together at his chest.	**MIA** OK, let's do this…I choose…uhm…I pick O, Oh, um, Olivia! (**Pauses.**)
Donovan and Mia exit STAGE RIGHT.	**REPORTER** Unbelievable! Ollie goes to Donovan's team with the last pick. (**To Ollie**) Ollie, can I have an exclusive interview?
Ollie exits STAGE RIGHT.	**OLLIE** (**Depressed**) I'm not in the mood to talk. I'm just going to go play ball.

Reporter follows Ollie offstage.

REPORTER
Ollie, how does it feel to be the worst kickball player at your school? **(Pauses.)** Ollie…*Ollie?*

FOR DEEPER LEARNING

SAY: ***Ollie must be feeling awful now—picked last again. Everyone wants to be great at everything. But we all seem to be good at just a couple of things.*** Read Romans 12:6-8.

Have children form groups of three or four and discuss:

- *Have you ever felt like Ollie? How did you handle those feelings?*

- *Why do you think God only gives us a couple of gifts that we are good at?*

- *What's your favorite gift that God gave you?*

- *How can you help others know that they're special instead of making them feel rejected or left out?*

Improv at the Cafeteria

Being Ridiculed: *Ephesians 4:29-32*

Cast:

CAFETERIA WORKER: an insecure guy trying to keep his dignity

FAST FREDDIE: a polished veteran comic on the cafeteria circuit

SILLY SALLY: a newcomer to comedy with an act that needs polishing

HECKLER: an offstage voice

Costuming: All characters wear street clothes. Cafeteria worker wears a hair net.

Props: A spatula, paper, and an "applause" sign

Setup: Fasten the spatula to the edge of the center stage to look like a microphone. Give each child a sheet of paper. Have a puppeteer hold up the "applause" sign when indicated.

SCRIPT

ACTIONS	WORDS
PLAY TRACK 7 ON CD B.	
Cafeteria worker enters and moves to CENTER STAGE.	**CAFETERIA WORKER** (**Gruff voice throughout skit**) Welcome. I'm the lunchroom cook, and I dish up more than soggy hamburgers. I run the Cafeteria Comedy Club. The principal thought it would be smart to distract you kids from looking at your plates.
Show applause sign.	Here's how we dish up the comedy. If a comedian is doing a good job, we'll hold up an applause sign and you clap your hands off. Try that. (**Pauses.**)

That was great. Occasionally we get a bad comic. If we get one today, I'm going to come out and ask you to crumple up your paper and throw it on stage. OK? **(Pauses.)**

Why not throw tomatoes? Well, you threw tomatoes last week. The principal saw me scrape the tomatoes off the floor and put them in that casserole you all loved. He *wasn't* too happy.

Now without further ado, I bring you Fast Freddie!

FAST FREDDIE
(With a quick bantering pace throughout) Thank you, thank you. It's good to be here with you all today.

Hey! Here's one for you…What did the cafeteria cook use to catch that fish you're eating? **(Pauses two beats.)**

Give up? His hair net.

Thank you, thank you. What do you get when you cross a dead skunk and a sack of potatoes? **(Pauses a beat.)** Why are you asking me? You ate it here last Friday. *Hey!*

CAFETERIA WORKER
(Offended) Hey, *yourself!* That was a possum, not a skunk.

FAST FREDDIE
(Continuing monologue) Why hasn't the health department closed this place down? **(Pauses two beats.)** Because there's no proof that they actually serve *food* here! *Hey, Hey!*

Fast Freddie enters from STAGE RIGHT and moves in front of the spatula at CENTER STAGE. Cafeteria Worker moves to UPSTAGE RIGHT and listens.

Show applause sign.

Show applause sign.

Show applause sign.

Freddie is taking bows.

Cafeteria Worker edges his way in front of Fast Freddie and speaks into the microphone.

Fast Freddie leans to the left from behind Cafeteria Worker so the kids can see him.

Cafeteria Worker turns his head to the left.

Fast Freddie exits STAGE LEFT shaking his head.

Silly Sally enters from STAGE RIGHT.

Cafeteria Worker returns to UPSTAGE RIGHT and watches Sally.
Cafeteria Worker quietly winces and shakes his head with every joke.

CAFETERIA WORKER
(**To himself**) I'm becoming the laughingstock of the school. The kids will make fun of me forever. I've got to do something.

(**To audience**) *Well*, that was just great, Fast Freddie. Thanks for joining us.

FAST FREDDIE
(**Confused**) I have more jokes. The crowd loves me. I'm not *done* yet.

CAFETERIA WORKER
(**Aside, to Fast Freddie, in a firm voice**) I'm afraid you are. *Done* is exactly what you are. (**Warmly, to audience**) Give a big round of applause for Fast Freddie!

I'd like to introduce a new comic to you. (**Emphatically**) Introducing, *Silly Sally!*

SILLY SALLY
(**Nervously**) Thank you…Thank you very much. Uhm…(**Stumbling**) I have a few jokes to tell you…a…Why did the dog stop using the sandpaper? (**Pauses.**)

It was giving him a "ruff" time.

(**Pauses.**) Get it? Sandpaper is rough. A dog says "ruff." (**Weakly**) It's a play on words…

OK, no sandpaper jokes. Let's see. Why did the chicken cross the road?

HECKLER'S VOICE
(**Shouting**) We've *heard* this one before! Come on!

SILLY SALLY

(Less confident) OK. Fair enough. Let me think...OK, this will work...Two chipmunks go into a gas station. Wait, that's not right. They go into a restaurant...and they weren't chipmunks, they were iguanas...I have this all *wrong.* Let me start over.

HECKLER'S VOICE

(Hollering) We want Fast Freddie! The cafeteria food is better than your jokes.

SILLY SALLY

(Rattled, talking to herself) Uhm...the food. That should get a laugh.

(Composed, to audience) Did you hear the one about the school's spaghetti?

Silly Sally moves to Cafeteria Worker.

CAFETERIA WORKER

(Whispering to Silly Sally) Pssst! What are you doing? I've been humiliated already. No food jokes.

SILLY SALLY

(Panicked) They hate me. I *need* the lunchroom jokes.

Cafeteria Worker pushes Silly Sally toward the microphone.

CAFETERIA WORKER

You get out there and be funny. I don't care *how* you do it.

SILLY SALLY

But, but...(Shakily) *Hey!* Why did the baseball player stare at his house?

(Pauses.) He wanted to see a home run.

(Several seconds of silence)

Get it. Home run?

SKIT SEVENTEEN:
Improv at the Cafeteria

HECKLER'S VOICE
(Angry) You're no good! Get off the stage.

Cafeteria Worker quickly moves to the microphone.

CAFETERIA WORKER
(Laughing weakly) Easy…easy there. Not everyone can be funny. I want you to tell her how you feel. Crumple your paper into a ball. On the count of three, I want you to throw it on the stage. Ready?

One…two…three.

(Pauses.)

Sally frantically shakes her head "no."

SILLY SALLY
(Crying) I made a complete fool out of myself. No one thinks that I'm funny.

Sally runs off sobbing STAGE LEFT. Cafeteria Worker watches her and moves to CENTER STAGE.

CAFETERIA WORKER
(Remorseful) Now I did it. I *humiliated her*. She feels awful. I just wanted people to laugh at her instead of *me*.

Cafeteria Worker turns his head and looks STAGE LEFT.

You kids have got to help me. What should I say to her? Turn to a friend, and try and think of something I could say that would help. I'll wait.

Cafeteria Worker addresses the children.

OK, you've come up with some pretty good ideas. I've got to go apologize to Silly Sally. When I see you tomorrow, I'll be serving meatloaf made with leftovers from the worms you dissected today. You'll love it.

Cafeteria Worker turns and exits STAGE LEFT.

FOR DEEPER LEARNING

SAY: *No one likes to be ridiculed. When a group of people make fun of you, it's hard to take. That's why God wants us to be careful with the types of words we use.* Read Ephesians 4:29-32.

Have children form groups of three or four and discuss:

- *When others make fun of you, how do you feel?*

- *Why do you think the Holy Spirit is sad when mean words are spoken?*

- *How can words build people up?*

- *Where can you use encouraging words this week?*

SKIT SEVENTEEN:
Improv at the Cafeteria

A Mouthful of Fear

Fear of Dentists and Doctors: *Isaiah 41:10*

Cast:

NORTON: himself

ZIPPY: a nervous, high-strung guy who is very afraid of the dentist

MAX: a mischievous character who likes to tease but has a fear of his own

ALICE: a kindhearted peacemaker

Costuming: All characters wear street clothes.

Props: Several extra children's clothes including shirts and socks and the largest pair of underwear you can find

Setup: Set the extra clothing within reach behind stage right.

SCRIPT

ACTIONS	WORDS
PLAY TRACK 8 ON CD B.	
Norton ENTERS and crosses to CENTER STAGE.	**NORTON** Boys and Girls, I don't want to alarm you. But this is the scariest skit that our troupe has done. Today's show is called "The Phantom Dentist." Because this is a scary show, keep a close eye on the adults. Make sure that they aren't too frightened.

You also need to have a buddy in case you get frightened. Now tell your friend about *your* first trip to the dentist or doctor's office. How did you feel? Talk about it. I'll wait…

Great stuff! Could you help me out? We spent so much money on organ music that we ran out of special effects money. Could you make the sound of a drill when you hear the word *dentist*? Let's try…*dentist*. **(Pauses.)** That's great! Well we're ready for the show. Without any further ado, I offer you "The Phantom Dentist!"

Norton exits.

As Zippy talks about the clothing he needs to pack, a puppeteer tosses those articles of clothing into the air from behind STAGE RIGHT.

ZIPPY
(From offstage, frustrated) I'm going to need this shirt…
…and those pants…
… gotta pack this…
… I'm going to need some underwear…

OK. I've got all of the clothes I'm going to need for my trip. Now I need some food. *Ouch!* My tooth hurts. I had better pack soft foods like applesauce. Off to the fridge…

Zippy enters from STAGE RIGHT. Zippy looks up and notices Alice offstage on STAGE LEFT.

Hi, Alice. What's up?

ALICE
(Inquisitively) Why are you packing your bags? You have a dentist **(pauses)** appointment in a few hours.

Alice enters from STAGE LEFT and notices the clothing all around.

ZIPPY
I'm not going. I've decided I need to see the world.

Zippy holds his hand against the side of his face.

Oh, this tooth is *killing* me! But, I'm not going to the dentist. **(Pauses.)** Call the office. Tell them I won't be there.

SKIT EIGHTEEN:
A Mouthful of Fear

ALICE
(**Sharply**) I will not! Call the dentist's (**pauses**) office yourself.

ZIPPY
(**Apprehensive**) No way. They get *vicious* if you cancel an appointment. Max told me about the dentist. (**Pauses.**) *That's* why I'm skipping town.

Oh, what a toothache!

ALICE
(**Accusingly**) *Max!* I wonder what horrible dentist (**pauses**) stories he told Zippy.

You! What did you tell Zippy? He's trying to run away.

MAX
(**Sheepish**) Ummm…I *did* tell him some scary dentist (**pauses**) stories.

Shouldn't we be trying to stop Zippy?

ZIPPY
(**Offstage, muffled voice**) I'm stuck in this closet. I need some help.

ALICE
(**Calling**) I know you are safe in there. I'll let you out when I'm done with *Max*.

(**To Max**) Well, what *did* you tell him?

ZIPPY
(**Offstage, muffled voice**) Tell her about the Phantom Dentist! (**Pauses.**)

ALICE
(**Sharply**) The what?

MAX
(**In an ominous voice**) The Phantom Dentist! (**Pauses.**)

Zippy exits STAGE RIGHT.

Alice moves to CENTER STAGE and faces audience.

Alice turns STAGE LEFT.

Max enters STAGE LEFT.

Alice turns her head to STAGE RIGHT.

Alice faces Max.

Alice spins and faces Max.

MAX

The Phantom Dentist (**pauses**) is a *sinister* fellow—seeking to drill holes in the teeth of young children. He doesn't use Novocain. He loves pain!

ZIPPY

(**Screams.**) You see! I can't go to the dentist. (**Pauses.**) He's going to attack my mouth with a buzz saw. Nothing can make me leave this closet. *OUCH!* Not even this tooth!

ALICE

(**To Zippy**) He will *not* attack your mouth with a buzz saw. The dentist (**pauses**) is a nice man. That tooth of yours sounds like it's really starting to hurt. You need to see the dentist. (**Pauses.**)

(**To Max**) Fix this. *You* got him all worked up. Say something to calm him down!

MAX

OK...OK...Calm down. I have it under control.

Zippy, look, I was just teasing when I said the Phantom Dentist (**pauses**) used a buzz saw on his patients. It's *not* true. (**Melodramatically**) He uses a jackhammer! (**Laughs sinisterly.**)

ZIPPY

(**Panicked**) No! There's no way I'm going. No! No! No—*Owie! My tooth, my tooth!*

ALICE

(**Sympathetically**) Come on out of there, Zippy. That tooth of yours really needs to be looked at, today.

Alice moves to STAGE RIGHT and faces RIGHT.

Alice moves to CENTER STAGE and faces Max.

Max moves to STAGE RIGHT and calls offstage.

Alice moves to the edge of STAGE RIGHT and moves her hand as if to open a door.

SKIT EIGHTEEN:
A Mouthful of Fear

Alice steps back to CENTER STAGE. Zippy enters from STAGE RIGHT with his hand on his mouth.

Stop listening to Max. He's just teasing—he just doesn't know when to stop. In fact, Max is afraid of going to the doctor's office.

ZIPPY
Realee, Maxth ith afraith of doctho's? Oh, thit toof is really aching.

MAX
Do we really need to talk about this now?

ALICE
I think it's only fair. **(Increasingly dramatic)** Once upon a time, Max was very sick. Max was nervous about the doctor's office, the metal scalpels, and the cold, *cold* stethoscope.

Max shudders.

MAX
(Shivers.) Brrrrrrr. I hate the stethoscope. And the doctor's office smells funny too.

ZIPPY
Why are you afraith? Dere's nuffing to be afraith of…it's just a docthor's offithe. **(Groans.)** Maybe, I *should* geth this loothked at.

Max begins to fidget uncomfortably.

ALICE
Max's brothers made up a story about **(melodramatically)** the Zombie Doctor of Hicksville. Why don't you tell Zippy about how your brothers frightened you?

MAX
(Nervous) Well, look at the time. It's getting late. I'd better be going now…

Max hurriedly exits STAGE LEFT.

Alice turns and faces STAGE LEFT.

ALICE
(Calling) It serves you right for frightening Zippy.

Alice turns and faces Zippy.

Zippy, you *really* need to see the dentist. **(Pauses.)** I'll go with you.

ZIPPY

(Groaning) Well, othay! I'm still nervous. But, *oh*, thith toof hurth!

ALICE

We'll see the dentist. (Pauses.) Then we'll stop by Max's house to calm him down.

ZIPPY

(From offstage) But the tooth fairy is real, right? Right?

Alice and Zippy exit STAGE LEFT

FOR DEEPER LEARNING

SAY: *Did you know that part of the Bible was written by a doctor? Dr. Luke wrote two books of the Bible, Luke and Acts. Dr. Luke was a good guy so maybe other doctors are OK too. And the Bible gives us a number of other verses that can comfort us when we're afraid of doctors or when we're sick. One verse you might remember when you're feeling afraid is Isaiah 41:10.* Read Isaiah 41:10 aloud.

Have children form groups of three or four and discuss:

- *Why do you think people get nervous going to the doctor or dentist?*

- *Was Alice justified in teasing Max about his fears? Why or why not?*

- *If you were one of Zippy's friends, what advice could you give him?*

- *What are other verses from the Bible that you can remember when you're feeling afraid because of the doctor or the dentist?*

SKIT EIGHTEEN:
A Mouthful of Fear

Holed Up

Fear of War and Terrorism: Psalm 46:1

Cast:

KIPP: a very serious person who is fearful at times

RICO: an adventure seeker

MOLLY: a southern belle and newly elected president of the Tree Frog Club

GRANDPA LEO: a wise and gentle grandfather who's seen a lot in his day

Costuming:
All characters wear street clothes. Grandpa Leo wears a cardigan sweater, a pair of wire glasses, and if possible, a gray wig.

Props: none

Setup: none

SCRIPT

ACTIONS	WORDS
PLAY TRACK 9 ON CD B.	
Grandpa Leo enters from STAGE LEFT. Grandpa Leo looks around searching.	**GRANDPA LEO** (**Puzzled**) Where is that noise coming from? All of that confounded banging and rattling... Why it sounds like it's coming from my basement. But I don't see anything. Maybe a skunk fell down the laundry bin again. I'd better go check.
Grandpa Leo exits STAGE RIGHT. Molly enters from STAGE LEFT and crosses to CENTER STAGE. She looks back over her shoulder toward STAGE LEFT.	**MOLLY** (**With a southern accent**) All right, that's enough for now. Lemonade break! We'll pick this up in ten minutes.

Kipp and Rico enter STAGE LEFT.

If Kipp is right, then we don't have much time to finish this bunker. We need this underground fortress before we're invaded.

KIPP

What do you mean *if* I'm right? Last night on the evening news a man said that the National Terror Alert is now "Code Orange." Our government believes that terrorists might attack us soon. We have to be ready for anything.

RICO

I need to have some questions answered before I do anything else. What are terrorists, and why would they want to attack us?

And do you think it's a good idea to be building a bunker in Grandpa Leo's basement?

KIPP

The terrorists are angry at our government. They don't agree with how our leaders run our country. Terrorists try to change things by scaring their enemies with bombs, guns, and other scary weapons. Instead of fighting our army, they choose to fight innocent people.

MOLLY

(**Urgently**) *That* is why we must finish this unda' ground room. We'll build the walls so thick that the terra'ists *can't* get to the Tree Frog Club.

Grandpa Leo will be grateful that we made a safe place that he can hide in afta' the terra'ists attack.

RICO

(**Doubting**) You mean that they can attack us *here*, in our little town? That would mean that no one is safe.

I don't believe it. You're mistaken. Maybe they were talking about the color orange and not "Code Orange." Maybe they are adding orange crayons to the box of 195 crayons or having a sale on orange juice.

KIPP

(**Insistent**) I know what I heard. Today's newspaper carried a ton of stories about terrorists. The president has even declared a war on terror.

Everybody is talking about it! I bet that even those kids out there have heard about terrorists and wars.

(**To children**) Kids, grab a partner, and share what you've heard about terrorists.

RICO

OK, OK! I trust these kids. They've heard about the terrorists too. I guess we *could* get attacked.

How long can we live in this bunker? I mean we need food, don't we? I'm willing to donate a twenty-pound bag of dog food that I have in my basement.

MOLLY

I'm certainly not eatin' dawg food, sweetie. No sir-ee! As president of the Tree Frog Club, I spent all of our club savings on nutritious and delicious food for our lil' bunka'. Boys, I bought enough canned oatmeal to last us a month.

Grandpa Leo enters STAGE RIGHT. Grandpa Leo jumps frightened.

RICO

Yuck! Canned oatmeal? *Gross!* That's enough to make me want to take my chances with the terrorists!

KIPP

Don't *say* that! Terrorists have all kinds of weapons. I read that they have chemical weapons that can make people sick. I'm worried.

GRANDPA LEO
(**Startled**) Bah!

Kipp, Rico, Molly! What are you three doing in my basement? You just about scared an old man half to death! What's the meaning of this? Why are you making such a racket?

MOLLY

Gran'pa Leo, we'ah trying to make a safe place to hide in when the terra'ists attack. We thought you'd be happy.

KIPP

Yeah, we added three feet of thickness to your walls by pouring concrete. Nothing will be able to get to you down here.

RICO

Please don't be mad at us. We're *terrified.* We don't want to die.

Molly and Kipp nod their heads in agreement.

MOLLY

(**Apologetic**) That's right. Don't be mad. We'll share our *canned oatmeal* with you. We have enough cans to stack from floor to ceiling.

GRANDPA LEO

Canned oatmeal? Yuck! Let's calm down and sort this out.

SKIT NINETEEN:
Holed Up

RICO

Aren't *you* worried at all?

GRANDPA LEO

Sure I get worried sometimes. But, I've lived through scary times before...like the Cold War.

RICO

(**Confused**) *Cold War?* Were you alive before guns were invented? Did you have to fight with snowballs?

GRANDPA LEO

(**Chuckling**) Very *funny*. During the Cold War, everyone was worried about nuclear bombs falling from the sky.

MOLLY

That's terra-bull. What ever did people do?

GRANDPA LEO

Back then some people built bunkers the way that you are. Children used to practice hiding underneath their desks at school. Some people, they just flat out panicked.

MOLLY

What *did* you do?

GRANDPA LEO

Me? I *prayed* a lot. I asked God for help. My favorite verse was Psalm 46:1: "God is our refuge and strength, an ever-present help in trouble."

A refuge is like a bunker...

RICO

(**Interrupting**) So are you saying that we don't *need* a bunker?

GRANDPA LEO

I don't know if you are going to need a bunker or not. I don't know if terrorists will attack or not. I *do* know two things.

I know that we can run to God whenever things are scary. I also know that you can't build a bunker in my house. You're going to have to fix that room and get your stuff out of here.

I'll be upstairs making some cookies. You can have some when you are done cleaning up.

Grandpa Leo exits STAGE RIGHT.

KIPP

Aw, *man*. Now what are we going to do? I guess we should have asked before we started building.

Kipp exits with his head down, discouraged.

RICO

I know! We can line the walls of our treehouse with cement. We'll have the world's first treehouse bunker.

Rico exits excited.

MOLLY

(Calling after Rico) That's a good idea. Just make sure we have enough room for the canned oatmeal. Let's go!

Molly quickly follows after him.

FOR DEEPER LEARNING

SAY: *The news is full of stories about terrorism and war. It's easy to get nervous about war or attacks in our country. But God is like a bunker. Let me read Grandpa Leo's favorite verse.* Read Psalm 46:1.

Have children form groups of three or four and discuss:

- *What worries you most about terrorists?*

- *Why wasn't Grandpa Leo as worried as the others?*

- *How can God be like our fortress when we hear scary news on TV?*

Homecoming

Parents: *Ephesians 6:1-2*

Cast:

    NORTON: himself

      PA: a grandpa who is hard of hearing and loves to tell tales of the good old days

      MA: a grandma who has gotten more compulsive about neatness as she ages

Costuming: Ma and Pa both wear wire-rimmed glasses, gray wigs, and flannel shirts. Norton wears street clothes.

Props: none

Setup: none

SCRIPT

ACTIONS	WORDS
PLAY TRACK 10 ON CD B. Ma and Pa enter STAGE LEFT. They move slowly and shuffle. Ma lowers herself a few inches.	**MA** Come on, Pa. It's almost time for Norton to be here. Let's take our seats. **PA** **(Straining to hear)** Beets? I don't want to eat beets. Besides, Norton is coming to visit us. I don't want to have beet-breath. **MA** **(Louder)** No, Pa! *Seats.* Why don't you sit down.

Norton enters STAGE RIGHT and hesitates.

Norton moves DOWNSTAGE and addresses the children.

Norton crosses to STAGE LEFT and stands next to Ma and Pa.

PA
Oh, I *understand.* I've got to get this hearing aid looked at. I think I will sit down. *Hey,* do we have any beets in the refrigerator? I'm hungry.

NORTON
(**Mumbling to himself**) Boy I hope this visit goes better than the last one. It's so hard to get along with my folks.

(**To kids**) Hey, kids. Boy, am I glad you are here. I'm about to visit my parents here at the retirement center. Man, these visits can be rough. My parents still treat me like a kid sometimes.

(**Pondering**) Like a kid…hmmm. You know. I have an idea. *You're* kids. You must be *experts* at getting along with parents. Being a grown-up myself, I'm a little out of practice. But *you*, you do this every day.

Turn to a nearby buddy, and tell that person what it's like having to get along with your parents every day. I'll wait.

Wow, you all have a lot of experience dealing with parents. Come visit with me. I'll turn to you for advice when things get sticky.

Hi, Mom. Hi, Dad. It's me, Norton. I've come to visit you.

MA
Norton! We're so glad to see you. How have you been?

NORTON
I'm doing fine, Mom. It's good to be here. (**Sniffing the air**) I think I smell cherry pie. That's my favorite.

SKIT TWENTY:
Homecoming

PA
(Alarmed) A hairy fly? *Where?* Don't just stand there, Norton! Get the fly swatter…

MA
(Loudly) No dear. Not "hairy fly." He said "cherry pie."

(To Norton) Sit down, dear.

Oh, not *there*, dear. I didn't have a chance to cover that chair with plastic. You might get cherry pie on the couch.

NORTON
(Surprised) One second, I'll be right back.

(To Children) Kids, OK. I need your help now. Do you see what's going on? My mom is a neat freak! Are your parents all focused on stuff like neatness? Talk to your buddy about how you deal with your mom and dad wanting to have a neat house.

OK, I guess all parents care about that stuff. I think Mom is being too careful about her couch. Parents can be so hard to live with. I guess I can keep the peace and sit on the chair.

PA
(Loudly) Who were those friends you were talking to? Are you hanging out with the right friends? Don't think that I've forgotten about the time when you and Stinky Henderson filled my toilet up with Jell-O!

NORTON
Dad, that was twenty years ago. **(Getting frustrated)** I've grown up. I know how to pick my friends.

(Calming down) I'll be right back.

Norton lifts up a bit and begins to drop two inches.

Norton moves to CENTER STAGE and addresses kids.

Norton moves to STAGE LEFT and sits on a chair.

Norton moves to CENTER STAGE.

(To kids, frustrated) Bah! Parents are always worried about the kinds of friends we choose. Why do you think that is? Ask your buddy why he or she thinks parents are always so worried about the friends we choose. I'm not going anywhere, I'll wait.

Time's up.

(Sighs.) You all have some good points. But, *boy* it's hard to get along with parents!

MA
So tell us what's happening in your life these days, Norton. Tell us everything.

NORTON
OK, well, I've been really busy with my work…

PA
(Interrupting) Busy with work? You don't know busy. Back in my day, we had to walk to work, uphill, both ways. We didn't have hammers. If we wanted to drive a nail into a board, we had to head butt it until the nail went into the wood. We worked long, long days. When I was a kid, a day was forty-eight hours long.

If you want my advice…

NORTON
(Interrupting) Advice? I didn't *ask* for advice. I didn't even get to tell you about my job. **(Trying to calm down)** Hold that thought, I'll be right back.

Norton walks back to Ma and Pa and sits down.

Skit Twenty:
Homecoming

Norton moves to CENTER STAGE.

(To children, with building frustration) It is so *hard* to deal with parents sometimes. Do your parents constantly give you advice that you *don't* want and tell you stories about when they were a kid? Why do they do that? Tell your friend why you think parents are always so quick to give advice.

Time's up. Hmmm, parents don't want us to repeat the mistakes they made? I guess that makes sense. I guess I just am tired of being treated like a kid. **(Sighs.)** I can do this…I can listen to Pa's advice.

MA
(Scolding) Now Norton, I've *asked* you not to sit on the couch.

NORTON
Oops, sorry Mom…

Norton returns to Ma and Pa and sits down.

(Hesitantly) I know, maybe I could take you both to a movie. Is there something you wanted to see?

Norton pops up, moves over a foot, and sits again.

MA
How sweet of you! There *is* a movie we've wanted to see. It's about parents who have the *worst* time raising their boy.

PA
Oh, I've wanted to see that movie for the longest time. No offense, Norton, but kids can be so *hard* to get along with.

Yoo-hoo! We're going to the movies! We'll meet you at the car, Norton.

Pa and Ma get up and exit STAGE LEFT. Norton moves UP CENTER STAGE as he talks.

NORTON
(In disbelief) What? *Kids* are hard to get along with?

(**To audience**) Kids, this whole getting along with your parents thing can be a big challenge. But I have to admit that I love my mom and dad.

I'm off to the movies! Thanks for the advice, and I hope things work out with your families.

Norton exits STAGE LEFT.

FOR DEEPER LEARNING

SAY: *Sometimes it can be hard to get along with our parents. But God not only wants us to get along with our parents, he wants us to honor them.* Read Ephesians 6:1-2.

Have children form groups of three or four and discuss:

* *What's the easiest part of getting along with parents? the hardest part?*

* *Why do you think God blesses people who honor their parents?*

* *How do you think your parents would feel if you treated them with honor? How would you feel doing it?*

* *What actions honor our parents?*

EVALUATION FOR

Instant Puppet Skits:
The Big Hairy Issues Kids Face

Please help Group Publishing, Inc., continue to provide innovative and useful resources for ministry. Please take a moment to fill out this evaluation and mail or fax it to us. Thanks!

Group Publishing, Inc.
Attention: Product Development
P.O. Box 481
Loveland, CO 80539
Fax: (970) 292-4370

● ● ●

1. As a whole, this book has been (circle one)
   not very helpful   *very helpful*
   1   2   3   4   5   6   7   8   9   10

2. The best things about this book:

3. Ways this book could be improved:

4. Things I will change because of this book:

5. Other books I'd like to see Group publish in the future:

6. Would you be interested in field-testing future Group products and giving us your feedback? If so, please fill in the information below:

Name _____

Church Name _____

Denomination _____ Church Size_____

Church Address _____

City   State   ZIP

Church Phone _____

E-mail _____

the 1 thing™

that everyone craves.

that really matters.

that gets undivided attention.

that can transform your life.

that encourages pastors.

that will re-energize you.

that will bring you joy.

that will unite your community.

that brings families closer.

that frees you.

that gives you focus.

that answers the why's.

that means true success.

that eliminates distractions.

that gives you real purpose.

that can transform your church.

Discover how *The 1 Thing* can revolutionize the way you approach ministry. It's engaging. Fun. Even shocking. But most of all, it's about re-thinking what "growing a relationship with Jesus" really means. Pick up Thom & Joani Schultz's inspiring new book today.

Thom & Joani Schultz

the 1 thing

What everyone craves—
that your church can deliver

13 LESSONS & Songs for Young Children

audio **CD** included

Simple Stories JESUS TOLD

Mary Rice Hopkins